Gay and Lesbian Theologies
Repetitions with Critical Difference

ELIZABETH STUART
King Alfred's College, Winchester

ASHGATE

Published by
Ashgate Publishing Company
Gower House
Croft Road
Aldershot
Hants GU11 3HR
England

Ashgate Publishing Company
Old Post Road
Brookfield, VT 05401–5600 USA

Ashgate website: http://www.ashgate.com

British Library Cataloguing in Publication Data
Stuart, Elizabeth, 1963-
   Gay and lesbian theologies : repetitions with critical
   difference
   1. Homosexuality - Religious aspects - Christianity 2. Gay
   men - Religious life 3. Lesbians - Religious life
   I. Title
   261.8'35'766

Library of Congress Cataloging-in-Publication Data
Stuart, Elizabeth, 1963-
      Gay and lesbian theologies : repetitions with critical difference/Elizabeth Stuart.
         p. cm
      Includes bibliographical references and index.
      ISBN 0-7546-1658-4 (hardcover) -- ISBN 0-7546-1661-4 (pbk.)
         1.Homosexuality--Religious aspects--Catholic Church.2.Catholic Church--Doctrines.
   I. Title

   BX1795.H66 S78 2002
   230'.086'64--dc21

                                                                    2002016327
ISBN 0 7546 1658 4 (Hbk)
ISBN 0 7546 1661 4 (Pbk)

Printed and bound by MPG Books Ltd., Bodmin, Cornwall.

Contents

Acknowledgements

I am grateful to King Alfred's College, Winchester for appointing me as the first Professor in Christian Theology, giving me the time, space and opportunity to reflect upon theology and sexuality and some study leave to complete this book. My colleagues and students in Theology and Religious Studies create a warm, supportive and intellectually rigorous environment in which to do theology. I am particularly grateful to my colleague David Sollis for his research on the Queering of Death project and for the constant theological and political debates/fights which have made me rethink a great deal of my own theology.

The Faculty of Divinity, Edinburgh University honoured me with the invitation to give the Cunningham Lectures in 2001 and I was able to share and discuss with staff and students the embryonic chapters of this book. Other organisations also invited me to give lectures in which I was able to test out some of the material that has made up this book and I am grateful to the Lesbian and Gay Christian Movement, the Modern Church People's Union, the International Marriage Conference, the Future of Theology Conference, the Universities of Essex and Reading and Westminster College, Oxford for the chance to share ideas with a wide range of people.

Much of my own work has been on friendship and I have been deeply grateful for the friendship of a number of people during the difficult year in which this book was written. Many people kept me going and I am especially thankful for the day to day support of Penny Cassell, Fr Kevin Michael, Stephen and Gwyneth Greenhalgh, Bishop Richard Palmer, Richard Kirker, Emma Barker-Knott, Jon Shephard, Robin Kuhnert, Bevan Robson, Christine Carter and Neil Stuart. My dear friend, Alan Bray, died shortly after I completed this book. Alan inspired much of my recent thinking on theology and sexuality and I am deeply grateful to have known him. My greatest debt is to Jane Robson and it is to her that this book is dedicated.

Chapter 1

Theological Trouble

What Happens to Lesbians when they Die?

I hope this lesbian will be dispatched according to the rites of the Roman Catholic Church. The *Order of Christian Funerals* approved for use in the dioceses of England, Wales and Scotland has a rich theology of death and I want to draw attention to two elements of the funeral rites. First, the rites are extremely hopeful. Neither hell nor even purgatory are allowed to cast their shadows over the coffin. The source of this hope for the deceased lies in their baptism, that is, in their status as persons initiated into the paschal mystery of Christ's death, resurrection and ascension. Indeed this is their only hope and the funeral rites constantly return to this fact not only in words but also in gestures and symbolism. The positioning of the Easter candle near the coffin recalls the Easter vigil in which the Church celebrates the paschal mystery into which Christians are baptised. Holy water sprinkled over the deceased at various points in the funeral rites 'remind the assembly of the saving waters of baptism' and 'its use calls to mind the deceased's baptism and initiation into the community of faith'.[1] Incense is used not only to symbolise the community's prayers for the deceased rising to God but 'as a sign of honour to the body of deceased, which through baptism became the temple of the Holy Spirit'.[2] A pall may be placed on the coffin as a reminder of the baptismal garment of the deceased and also as a symbol of the fact that all are equal in the eyes of God. The clear preference for liturgical colour (with due deference to local custom) is white which 'expresses the hope of Easter, the fulfilment of baptism and the wedding garment necessary for the kingdom'.[3] The Eucharist is the ordinary and principal celebration of the Christian funeral because it is the memorial of the paschal mystery and the place where the faith of the baptised in that paschal mystery is renewed and nourished.

Second, though the family and friends of the deceased are encouraged to play a significant part in the preparation and execution of the funeral rites there is a strong emphasis on the involvement of the whole local Christian community not only in offering a ministry of consolation but in active participation in the rites from the vigil to the committal, an involvement which has practical consequences in, for example, the timing of funerals.[4] The deceased belongs primarily to the Church of which the family is a subgroup. Other elements reinforce the priority of this ecclesial personhood. The general introduction is emphatic that 'there is never to be a eulogy' only a homily on the content of Christian hope.[5] Non-biblical readings are permitted only in prayer services with the family, not in the funeral Eucharist itself. Only Christian symbols such as a Bible or cross may be placed on or near the coffin as a reminder of the faith of the deceased, 'any other symbols, for example, national flags, or flags or insignia of associations, have no place in the funeral liturgy'.[6] All bonds, associations and worldly achievements pale into significance beside the status of the deceased as a baptised member of the body of Christ.

So, 'in the end' as the Church commits my whole person – body and soul – to God what will it teach those gathered to mourn my passing about my sexuality? The answer to that question is something so radical that the Church itself seems unable at the present time to digest its own teaching. The Church teaches that in the end all other identities other than that conveyed through baptism are relativised (which is not to say that they are dismissed as unimportant as the involvement of friends and family and the opportunity provided for some personal remembrance of the deceased in some rites indicates). There is only one identity stable enough to hope in. At death my Church teaches me that all my secular identities are placed under 'eschatological erasure' as Malcolm Edwards has put it.[7] They are not matters of ultimate concern. At my death all that has been written on my body will be once again overwritten by my baptism as it was a few weeks after my birth when I was immersed in the waters of death and rebirth and a new character was given to me which nothing can ever destroy. In the end before the throne of grace everything will dissolve except that identity. Gender, race, sexual orientation, family, nationality and all other culturally constructed identities will not survive the grave. They will pass away, the 'I' that is left, the I am that I am is not, as the popular song would have it, 'my own special creation' nor the creation of the human communities, the I am that I am is God's own special creation and that is my only grounds for hope.

Gordon Lathrop has argued that 'Christian liturgy orients its participants in the world'.[8] Liturgy provides the maps by which we interpret and navigate this world and the world to come. In the end the funeral liturgy of the Roman Catholic Church re-orientates its participants back to their baptism. This theology of baptism shakes the foundations upon which much gay and lesbian theology, and indeed most theological reflection on sexuality from all quarters, has been based in the last 30 years. For, as Mary McClintock Fulkerson has noted, what is remarkable about the debates around homosexuality in the western Churches is not so much the grounds of difference between participants as the unquestioned shared assumptions, in particular the modern discourses of sexual identity: 'Both those who refuse gay and lesbian persons and those who insist upon their inclusion in the life of the church share the idea that persons have a sexual identity and sexual preference and that this identity, for good or ill, is an absolutely fundamental status-determinative reality about subjects.'[9] It is this assumption that the theology of baptism challenges.

What Happens to Sodomites when they Die?

In canto 26 of part two of Dante's *Divine Comedy – Purgatory* Dante describes his experiences in the top cornice of upper purgatory, near to the earthly paradise from which humanity fell and which all the souls in the top cornice will eventually reach. The souls of those in the top cornice then are close to paradise. They consist of two groups of people running in opposite directions around the fiery cornice. One group circle the mountain from east to west (following the pattern of the sun as do all the rest of the souls on the mountain of purgatory), the other group uniquely run the opposite way. When they meet the souls exchange kisses and go on their way, but as they pass they name the sin from which they are being purged. One group shouts 'Sodom! Gomorrah!', the other at the same time, 'Into the cow Pasiphae/Leaps, that the bull may hasten to her lust'.[10] These are penitent Christians guilty of the sin of *luxuria*, the excessive, self-indulgent love of others. They have disordered their desire so that love for others has eclipsed their desire for God. A shade from what Dante calls the 'hermaphrodite' group explains that the other group 'went awry/In that for which Caesar of old heard "Queen!"/ Flung at him as he passed in triumph by... '.[11] The tone of this canto then is fairly light-hearted as befits the status of souls so near the end of their journey and the focus is not on the Sodomites who have violated Natural Law but the others who have violated Human Law by behaving like beasts in their lust.

There are three points I want to make about Dante's vision of the seventh cornice of purgatory. First, note how those guilty and repentant of excessive desire for others are placed on a higher cornice of purgatory than those guilty of gluttony or avarice, also examples of excessive desire, and how all these are sins ranked 'higher' that sloth or accide – defective love which fails to expend enough energy – and pride, envy and wrath, forms of perverted love, perverted because they centre on the self rather than others and God. For Dante then excessive desire for others is what Dorothy L. Sayers rather charmingly calls a 'warm-hearted' sin because it involves some sort of mutual exchange and reciprocity.[12] Second, note how all those guilty of sin of *luxuria* are in the same boat or rather on the same cornice. They might run in different directions just as in life they may have batted for different teams as one contemporary expression puts it but in purgation violators of the *Lex Naturalis* and *Lex Humana* are in the same place, engaged in the same act of purgation. Their brief exchange of kisses acknowledges their fellowship. Third, it is a theme of the *Divine Comedy* that love simultaneously propels and repels humans from the divine. When it is properly ordered love thrusts us into the heart of the divine mystery, when it is disordered, wrongly focussed, it turns our focus away from God. Yet love however perverted is capable of being redeemed, it always has the potential of being refocused. Like a navigator's compass it may need to be reset but without it there is no hope at all of finding one's way to God.

The *Divine Comedy* thrusts us back into a Christian world in which sexuality and gender and their relationship to the divine were constructed in very different terms than in our own western twenty-first century cultures. In an age when even the Roman Catholic Church has gone rather silent on the doctrine of purgatory (it is only implied in the funeral liturgy) the possibility that in the end all human love no matter to whom it is directed might only take us to the edge of heaven seems to have been replaced by the conviction that some forms of love i.e. heterosexual marriage carry us further than others. The idea that all love has its origins and its *telos* (end and fulfilment) in God has been replaced in much contemporary Church teaching on sexuality with the implicit or explicit teaching that all love has its *telos* in heterosexual marriage and, for some, the bringing of new life into the world from it. And the possibility that those who direct their loves in different directions might recognise and enjoy a fellowship based upon a penitent recognition of shared weaknesses and a desire for God seems totally alien much of the current debate on sexuality in the western Churches which has congealed around the 'issue' of homosexuality where lesbian and gay people, their supporters and their opponents currently slump exhausted, having gone too many brutal rounds with one another, barely able now to muster the energy to raise two fingers at each other never mind exchange a loving kiss.

On the 'issue of homosexuality' all sides have reached a state of theological breakdown. Mark Jordan has analysed the rhetorical devices employed by the Vatican in its teaching on homosexuality and identified one of those devices as tedium achieved through repetition.[13] Repetition of arguments creates the illusion of stability, immutability and naturalness. It falsifies history by drowning out counter arguments or different worldviews. My contention is that this analysis could be applied with equal force to the body of theology written by self-identified lesbian and gay Christians. The collapse into repetition is symptomatic of a failure of all sides to produce satisfactory theologies, theologies that engage, convince and change opponents. Michael Vasey has argued that what has caused this failure in much Church teaching on homosexuality is an unconscious adoption of the assumptions and values of modernity.[14] I want to argue that this is what has also blighted gay and lesbian theology.

I want to make clear at the outset that I do not think gay and lesbian theology has been a mistake. I have made a small contribution to that body of theology, a contribution of which I am proud and which I stand by. It is an ancient Christian belief that the divine speaks through all forms of knowledge. But at the same time as the divine speaks through a body of knowledge it also disrupts and subverts it, theology no less so than other forms of knowledge. I want to argue that gay and lesbian theology has achieved much but it has proved itself incapable of getting us to the seventh cornice of purgatory and what has prevented it from doing so is an uncritical buying into modern notions of sexual identity. Both gay and lesbian theology and much official Church teaching on homosexuality would flounder in the face of the theology of the Roman Catholic funeral liturgy or Dante's vision of purgatory. However, I believe that the newly emerging body of theology known as queer theology is able to engage creatively with this tradition and bring gay and straight together in the quest to take part in the redemption of sexuality precisely because it questions the notion of stable sexual identity. I also believe that instead of just feeding off secular knowledge queer theology has the potential to make a contribution to queer theory and rescue it from nihilism because the Church is the only community under a divine command and constructed according to a divine logic to be queer.

This then is going to be the argument of this book. Much of the book consists of a critical survey of the development of gay and lesbian theology. No theology, however, emerges in a vacuum and gay and lesbian theology has to be understood against two backgrounds – the development of Christian theology in the west in the latter half of the twentieth century and the development of gay and lesbian studies. Many of the weaknesses of gay and lesbian theology are weaknesses inherited from these two sources.

The Development of Christian Theology

Joerg Rieger has provided a useful model with which to make sense of the development of western Christian theology in the twentieth-century. He characterises the development of Christian theology as four 'turns'.[15] The first turn is the turn to the self, the defining characteristic of liberal theology which dominated British and North American theology in the twentieth century. Responding to the break down of metaphysics, liberal theology took the Enlightenment's notion of the autonomous, rational self and made that the point of contact between humanity and the divine. All human beings are believed to share common experiences and these become the road to the divine. Theology ceases to consist of reflection on the nature of God and becomes a hermeneutical enterprise reflecting on the meaning of human experience and Christian faith. Doctrine is understood as a symbolic articulation of human experience and constantly open to critique by that experience. Liberal theology has many strengths. Because it locates the point of contact between the divine and humanity in human experience it opens up the theological enterprise and enables people previously excluded from the processes of theology to make a contribution. It reminds us that doctrine and theology always have their origin in the context of peoples' lives. However, there are problems with liberal theology. Whilst it may present itself as a democratic and inclusive form of theology, the modern self upon which liberal theology is based is not the universal human self (which, of course, does not exist) but the middle class self which emerged from the Enlightenment claiming the right and ability to interpret the world. Charles Winquist said of the father of modern liberal theology Friedrich Schleiermacher, 'Schleiermacher constructed a definition of religion out of an experience that most of us have not had. Instead of being inclusive of what we might call religion, it now functions negatively, excluding experiences that cannot meet its measure'.[16] So whilst claiming to be inclusive liberal theology ends up doing violence to experiences that contradict or question the experience of the middle class self. Collapsing doctrine into the self's experiences renders the self incapable of being challenged or hoisted above its own horizons. Theology can be reduced to a form of narcissism.

The second turn in twentieth-century theology is the turn to the Other and this turn manifested itself in the neoorthodoxy of Karl Barth and his disciples. Neoorthodoxy is a conscious reaction against the turn to the self, the idolatry of which it was believed by Barth led to two world wars. Neoorthodoxy emphasises the radical difference between God and humanity. God is constructed as wholly other. Whereas liberal theology is fundamentally an apologetic theology justifying the place of Christian belief and practice in the modern world, neoorthodoxy concerns itself primarily with the internal workings of the Church and its tendency to fall into heresy which is the identification of the human with God whether that manifests itself in the liberal turn to the self or in doctrinalism. Theology must begin from the realisation that it itself is helpless, incapable of even asking the right questions still less of straddling the divide between the divine and the human. There is no natural point of contact between humanity and God. The only point of contact is God's word incarnate in Jesus Christ. Whilst drawing attention to the dangers of liberal theology and insisting on a proper humility in the process of doing theology which restored some awareness of the majesty and glory of God, neoorthodoxy also has its weaknesses. Unless respect for God's otherness is combined with a respectful consciousness of the otherness of human beings it is tempting to construct the otherness of God in one's own image so that the modern self is not dislocated but repressed. Furthermore, part of the attraction of the turn to the Other may well be a desire to escape from dealing with the harsh political realities of human otherness.

The turn to others constitutes the third turn. Theologies of liberation are, like liberal theology, rooted in experience, not the experience of the middle class self but the experience of conflict and a sense of cognitive dissonance, of disconnection between reality as presented and reality as experienced. Unlike liberal theology which cannot deal with the reality of conflict because it threatens to unmask the fiction of universal human experience and neoorthodoxy which is only concerned with the conflict between humanity and God, theologies of liberation begin in the reality of what hurts, of conflicts between human beings and it is there that God is encountered. Experience does not function foundationally as it does in liberal theology but rather as a reminder of the conflicts and power games that other forms of theology ignore or try and disguise. In theologies of liberation the theologian is acutely aware of their relationship to others and the possible misuse of their own power. In theologies of liberation notions of absolute truth are jettisoned in favour of a glimpse of truth encountered where relationships begin to be healed. Doctrine is a pointer to the truth and meaningful only to the point that it aids such healing. Because of an awareness of the power dynamics behind the formation of doctrine, doctrine is no longer limited to the formal statements of the Church. This third turn attempts to guard against the idolising of the self and attempts to make theology truly inclusive by adding more and more voices to it but it has a tendency to romanticise the position of the marginalized and whilst its aim is to constantly broaden theological horizons, ironically an awareness of the otherness of others can serve to ghettoise theologies of liberation into special interest groups.

The fourth turn is the turn to the text or postmodern theology. Theologians have responded to the end of the metanarrative which postmodernity brings in two different ways. There are those such as Mark C.Taylor who have taken postmodern philosophy as foundational and gleefully embraced the loss of truth, self and God that it brings, collapsing theology into religious studies, anthropology and cultural studies and spirituality into a nihilistic mysticism.[17] Then there are those such as the post-liberal and radical orthodoxy schools of theologians who have taken advantage of the eclipse of the metanarrative in order to reclaim a place for Christianity in public discourse and as a form of epistemology. In these theologies there is a recentralising of the texts of the Christian tradition which are understood to constitute the 'grammar' of the Church. Like neoorthodoxy these theologies exhibit enormous self-confidence in the Christian tradition but unlike neoorthodoxy they refuse to recognise any sort of dualism between faith and reason or grace and nature. There is no secular realm, no space beyond the divine and therefore no aspect of life which theology has not interest in or the ability to illuminate. The turn to the text sometimes suffers from a failure to engage with the power dynamics behind the text. It does not give much thought to the possibility that Christianity may have sometimes gone wrong.

These then are the four turns that took place in twentieth-century theology. What Rieger fails to make sufficiently clear is that whilst these four turns did occur in chronological succession they all continued and continue to exist. We shall see that three of these turns are evident in the body of work produced by self-identified gay and lesbian theologians who tend to replicate the general weaknesses of the approaches outlined above. The one turn that is not evident in gay and lesbian theology is the turn to the Other. This may be because Barth took the view that homosexuality was a 'physical, psychological and social sickness … [a] phenomenon of perversion, decadence and decay' which resulted from a contravention of a divine command – the command for male and female to exist in fellowship.[18] Indeed, Barth advocated a theory of the complementarity of the sexes that went further than the Roman Catholic Church could ever go because he believed that everything that segregated the sexes including religious orders was a direct disobedience of the divine command and itself likely to lead to homosexuality. Neoorthodoxy does not therefore look a very promising type of theology from a lesbian or gay perspective.

The Development of Gay and Lesbian Studies

As well as developing in and from the broad context of western Christian theology gay and lesbian theology has also developed against the backdrop of gay and lesbian studies and therefore it is important to outline the 'turns' that have taken place in this discipline because shifting understandings of sexuality have certainly impacted upon gay and lesbian theology.[19]

The Stonewall Riots of June 1969 – caused when the patrons of a New York bar known as a relatively safe space for the sexually marginalized resisted a routine police raid and fought back against the harassment for four days – have become the mythical and symbolic beginnings of the modern gay liberation movement. They are commemorated each year all over the western world and beyond in annual gay pride celebrations. Stonewall symbolises the transformation of homosexual people into lesbian and gay people as they claimed their own voice, subjectivity, moral agency and right to self-definition and determination. It also symbolises a rejection of heterosexual normativity and the pathologising of homosexuality. After Stonewall lesbians and gay men began to create a public cultural space for themselves and demand equality before the law and in society as a whole as a stable minority group. In other words what Stonewall represents is the creation of a gay or lesbian self. The act of 'coming out' became the ritual by which men and women claimed with pride an identity which others despised and in the process challenged and undermined the modern construction of the homosexual. A key target for the gay and lesbian studies that emerged from the gay liberation movement was the psychological construction of homosexuality as an illness. The experience of gay and lesbian people was presented as being far more authoritative than that of heterosexual 'experts'. In the early years of the gay liberation movement the social agenda was radical and included a deconstruction of traditional constructions of sexuality and gender to enable the emergence of the fundamentally bisexual nature of humanity and the reconstruction of sex as primarily a pleasurable rather than reproductive activity. However by the mid 1970s this liberationist agenda which was constructed on an understanding of human nature as fundamentally androgynous and polymorphous in its desire had by and large given way to a model of identity based upon an ethnic minority model and a political agenda aimed no longer at subverting the social order but reforming it through integration.

The lesbian feminist movement developed in parallel to the gay liberation movement among lesbians who felt marginalized in both gay liberation circles and in the woman's movement. In its early days this movement shared much of the vision of the gay liberation movement. Lesbianism tended to be understood less as a sexual orientation and more as a defiant way of being in a patriarchal world. One popular definition of a lesbian was 'a women-identified woman' which potentially included all women. It was to other women rather than to gay men that lesbian feminists tended to look for solidarity, gay men being regarded as implicated in the structures of patriarchy to the same degree as heterosexual men. The lesbian feminist movement also changed its focus in the 1970s when both movements became locked in venomous struggles over the limits of a 'proper' lesbian or gay identity. It was felt important to establish these limits because in order to invoke the rights of citizenship based upon an ethnic minority model, gay and lesbian people needed to project a coherent cultural voice. At the same time black lesbian and gays claimed a voice that called into question the notion of a unitary lesbian or gay self.

The 1970s also saw the birth of the essentialist versus social constructionist debate within gay and lesbian studies. Broadly speaking essentialists argue that a person's sexual orientation is an objective and transcultural fact. Though essentialists may disagree as to the origin of sexual orientation (some would attribute it to genetic make up, others to a person's first pleasurable encounter or to interaction with their parents) they would agree that homosexuality is a transcultural and transhistorical phenomenon. One of the most prominent advocates of essentialism was the gay Catholic historian John Boswell who sought to demonstrate in his historical works that there were times in pre-modern Europe when the Roman Catholic Church had been tolerant of same sex desire and even celebrated it in form of liturgical unions.[20] It is crucial to Boswell's wider apologetic agenda that there is at least some family likeness between twentieth-century gay people and those expressing desire for the same sex in pre-modern Europe.

Social constructionists, however, maintain that sexual orientation is culturally dependent and historically conditioned. Some maintain that it is possible to pinpoint the moment that the homosexual emerged in western culture, others maintain that rather like the category of witch in the seventeenth century, there are no real homosexuals (or indeed heterosexuals) because no one actually fits the script. Both types of social constructionists would deny that homosexuals existed in pre-modern times. They do not deny that there were people who engaged in same-sex sexual activity but this did not mark them out as a particular type of person, their sexual behaviour did not tell 'the truth' about them in the way that it does in western society today. Even a cursory exploration of contemporary non-western cultures reveals that different cultures construct and interpret desire in very different ways to North American and European cultures suggesting that sexual orientation is a social construction.

Undoubtedly the most prominent advocate of social constructionism was Michel Foucault. Foucault questioned the two central notions upon which post-Enlightenment theory and theology of sexuality have been based. The first is the notion of a fixed, essential identity, sexual or otherwise. Foucault argued for the social construction of sexual identity through discourse and constant redefinition. The second is the idea that power is something held by dominant groups and used against others who had less power e.g. women, gay people, the poor, etc. Foucault argued that power was fluid and present in all parts of society and could be deployed by any group. Where power was exercised there was always resistance to it, which itself was a kind of power.[21] It was Foucault who pinpointed the construction of the homosexual to around 1870 when medical discourse began to interpret same-sex sexual activity as evidence of a person's species. Others have since posited different dates and different causes for the invention of homosexuality. Alan Bray locates it at the end of the eighteenth century and the development of the culture of molly houses in London.[22] Whereas others such as Jeffrey Weeks and John D'Emilio attribute the emergence of homosexuality to the restructuring of the family that took place in the nineteenth century in the wake of the development of capitalism which enabled people to exist outside the family unit.[23] The social constructionist approach assumes not only the creation of the homosexual but also the creation of the heterosexual and heterosexuality and this is perhaps the most radical aspect of the social constructionist position. For homosexuality has been constructed as unnatural against an assumption of the naturalness of heterosexuality. The homosexual has been defined against the heterosexual. In social constructionism both homosexuality and heterosexuality are denaturalised, historicized and rooted in specific cultures.

Foucault died in 1984 with AIDS. AIDS was the great symbol and sacrament of post modernity. Not only did AIDS shake human confidence in the great metanarratives of science, medicine and human progress but it also revealed the hopeless inadequacy of modern notions of sexual identity. Those involved in safe sex campaigns soon found that men who had sex with men did not necessarily identify as gay and that categories of sexual identity proved a poor guide to people's sexual behaviour. AIDS literally and horrifically symbolised the death of the subject. The political response to AIDS, as well as the public perception of it, united groups that had previously emphasised their difference from one another – lesbians, gay men, bisexuals and transgendered persons. They adopted a new political identity 'queer' which challenged and subverted the sexual categories that informed the dominant discourses surrounding AIDS.

In 1990 two books, both by women, both deeply influenced by Foucault were published. These books herald the birth of queer theory. Eve Kosofsky Sedgwick in her book *Epistemology of the Closet*[24] analysed the competing discourses around sexuality in modern western thought. She identified two sets of conflicting discourses: the essentialist 'minoritising' understanding of homosexuality versus the 'universalising' understanding which regards sexual desire as a spectrum which allows for choice and a separatist attitude to gender versus an attitude that celebrates the liminality between genders. Sedgwick's analysis drew attention to the fact that modern homosexuality was not a stable, coherent identity but incoherent and contested.

Judith Butler in her book *Gender Trouble* set out to explore why gender has been such a troublesome issue in feminism.[25] She utilised Foucault's method of genealogical critique which is not interested in the origins or truths of things but in the reasons why people search for the origins and causes of sexual desire and the political implications and effects of such a search. Butler argued that feminism has made a fundamental error in continuing to assume that there is a stable identity of 'woman' somehow bound up with the female body which is stable enough to make some (though perhaps not many) generalizations about. This is a paradoxical position for most feminists to take, considering their antipathy to the 'biology is destiny' approach to gender. Butler sought to question the 'natural' connection between sex, gender and desire, arguing that gender and desire are unstable. Indeed, she famously asserted that gender is not expressive of some inner nature but peformative. We learn to become a woman or a man by following the gender scripts that our culture hands out to us and each performance reinscribes that gender upon our bodies. It is only when some people attempt to throw away the scripts or perform them badly or subversively that the non-natural nature of gender is revealed. Butler argued that the parodic performance of gender by drag queens or butch and femme lesbians most clearly demonstrated and disrupted the connection between sex, gender and performance. She called for a resistance to the gender scripts that are handed out to us and a proliferation of subversive performances of gender but noted the difficulty of resisting such scripts because no one stands completely outside of them. This is then the 'essence' of queer theory, that there is no essential sexuality or gender. 'Queer' then is not actually another identity alongside lesbian and gay (although it is sometimes rather confusingly used to convey a radical coalition of lesbian, gay, bisexual and transgendered persons[26]) but a radical destabilizing of identities and resistance to the naturalizing of any identity.

Queer theory is not without its critics. Some have argued that queer theory along with all postmodern theory far from being the radical, liberating analysis it claims to be is in fact conservative and patriarchal because it shows little interest in the reality of people's lives and too easily erases the identities that marginalized groups have fought to establish. Ki Namaste, for example, accuses queer theorists of trivialising the lives of transgendered people by constructing their sexuality in terms of gender play. This is not how most transgendered people would understand their sexuality nor their political struggle against violence and marginalisation.[27] As Susan Wolfe and Julia Penelope put it, 'in one hundred short years, German sexologists have "appeared" Lesbians in order to pathologies us and French poststructuralists have 'disappeared" us in order to deconstruct sex and gender categories and to "interrogate" the subject.'[28] Others have argued that queer theory though making sense intellectually cannot be translated into an effective political strategy where a political essentialism is called for. Still others have claimed that queer theory is inaccessible to those beyond the academy and has no roots in real communities and struggles. But undoubtedly what has worried lesbian and gay scholars and activists most about queer theory is that it seems to require a surrendering of lesbian/gay identity.

Theological Trouble

This book will offer a critical analysis of the development of lesbian, gay and queer theology against the twin backdrops of western Christian theology and gay and lesbian studies. Chapter two examines the theology that emerged in UK and the USA from self-identified lesbian and gay people in the aftermath of Stonewall. These works will be shown to be confident apologetics grounded in the methodologies and assumptions of liberal theology. The sexual agenda of these early works is sometimes liberationist, sometimes not. Chapter three focuses on the theology that emerged from the gay male theologians after the realisation dawned that lesbians and gay men do not share something that can be summed up as 'gay experience'. Some of these theologies draw upon the methodologies of theologies of liberation (particularly Latin American liberation theology), some upon a radical type of postmodern theology (such as is represented by Taylor) and some on both. Both essentialist and social constructionist approaches to sexuality are evident. The emergence of lesbian theology as a distinct body of theology is the subject of chapter four. Also drawing upon theologies of liberation (particularly feminist theology) and lesbian feminist theory this body of theology is largely social constructionist in approach and whilst generally advocating a liberationist sexual agenda nevertheless also exhibits some of the anxieties over the limits of identity evident in the wider lesbian feminist movement at the time.

In chapter five AIDS is used to test the claim of gay and lesbian theology to speak out of gay and lesbian experience. AIDS cast a pall of death over gay and lesbian people in the UK and USA (and elsewhere) during the 1980s and early 1990s before the advent of Combination Therapy slowed down the rates of death. This chapter will argue that whilst gay and lesbian theology achieved much, changing the face of Christian theology by deconstructing dominant heterosexist discourses, it failed to address adequately the cultural and theological issues raised by AIDS and as a result has since been able to do little else than repeat itself.

The remainder of the book charts the development of queer theology beginning in chapter six with an analysis of Robert Goss' book *Jesus Acted Up: A Gay and Lesbian Manifesto* (1993) which constitutes a bridge between the methodologies of gay and lesbian theology and that of queer theology being heavily influenced by Foucault. Chapter seven analyses the development of queer theology, its indebtedness to Butler and the radical break it signifies from the assumptions and methodologies of gay and lesbian theology. I will suggest that the queerest theology to date has come from the school of theology known as radical orthodoxy. Chapter eight will conclude the book by outlining a queer theology developing the themes of the previous chapter and arguing for the validity of a queer approach against its detractors. I will argue that it comes as near as any other theological reflection upon sexuality to getting us to the seventh cornice of purgatory.

The theme of repetition runs through the book. I have already intimated that one of my contentions is that gay and lesbian theology reached a state of theological breakdown and this manifested itself in a tendency to simply repeat itself (mirroring the repetitious discourse of those who oppose the inclusion of lesbian and gay people in the full life of the Christian community). Butler maintains that gender is inscribed upon the body through repetition. Queer theorists have argued that therefore it is necessary to perform gender – to repeat – with critical difference in order to subvert it. I want to argue that repetition with critical difference is at the heart of Christian praxis and therefore there is a kinship between queer and Christian and more, that Christian theology has the ability to prevent queer theory falling into repetitious nihilism. Christianity is a queer thing.

In French répétition has the meaning of rehearsal and I believe that it was absolutely necessary for gay and lesbian theology to come into being but only as a rehearsal, a preparation for something more theologically radical. In many ways this book charts the story of my own theological journey from my training in liberal theology through an embracing of liberation and feminist theology which led me to extensive involvement in theological and ecclesiastical debates around sexuality, through to a sort of theological breakdown caused by a realisation that we were actually getting nowhere, to an embracing of the queer approach and the development of queer theology which I believe, though it has its weaknesses, does have the possibility of not so much reviving a tired debate but bringing to birth a whole different and thoroughly theological approach to sexuality. In this book I will be critiquing my own previous work alongside that of others and when referring to my past work I speak of myself in the third person, not because I wish to disown that work but simply for the sake of clarity.

I am conscious of the inherent weaknesses of my approach. In seeking to survey and categorise gay and lesbian theology I will inevitably do violence to some of it. I cannot refer to all works published in this field and will only refer to those works published in English. Nevertheless I am convinced that the points I make are broadly valid and that they have a validity that often extends beyond gay and lesbian theology to twentieth century western theology in general.

Notes

1   *Order of Christian Funerals* (London: Geoffrey Chapman, 1990), para. 36.
2   *Order of Christian Funerals*, para. 37.
3   *Order of Christian Funerals*, para. 39.
4   *Order of Christian Funerals*, paras. 9–11.
5   *Order of Christian Funerals*, p. 8.
6   *Order of Christian Funerals*, p. 11.
7   Malcolm Stuart Edwards, 'Christianity and the Subversion of Identity: Theology, Ethics and Gay Liberation', PhD Thesis, Cambridge University, 1998, pp. 176–7.
8   Gordon Lathrop '"O Taste and See": The Geography of Liturgical Ethics', in E. Byron Anderson and Bruce T. Morrill (eds), *Liturgy and the Moral Self: Humanity at Full Stretch Before God* (Collegeville: Minnesota, 1998), p. 41.
9   Mary McClintock Fulkerson, 'Gender – Being it or Doing It? The Church, Homosexuality, and the Politics of Identity', in Gary David Comstock and Susan E. Henking (eds), *Que(e)ring Religion: A Critical Anthology* (New York: Continuum, 1999), p. 189.
10 Dante, *The Divine Comedy 2: Purgatory*, Canto XXVI (Harmondsworth: Penguin Books, 1955), pp. 272–3.
11 Dante, *The Divine Comedy 2: Purgatory*, Canto XXVI, p. 274.
12 Dorothy L. Sayers in her Introduction to Dante, *The Divine Comedy 2: Purgatory*, p. 67.
13 Mark Jordan, *The Silence of Sodom: Homosexuality in Modern Catholicism* (Chicago and London: University of Chicago Press, 2000), pp. 54–7.
14 Michael Vasey, *Strangers and Friends: A New Exploration of Homosexuality and the Bible* (London: Hodder and Stoughton, 1995).
15 Joerg Rieger, *God and the Excluded: Visions and Blindspots in Contemporary Theology* (Minneapolis: Fortress Press, 2001).
16 Charles E. Winquist, *Desiring Theology* (Chicago and London: University of Chicago Press, 1995), p. 4.
17 Mark C. Taylor, *Altarity* (Chicago: University of Chicago Press, 1987).
18 Karl Barth, *Church Dogmatics* III.4 (Edinburgh: T and T Clark, 1960), pp. 164–6.
19 The following texts provide surveys of the development of gay and lesbian studies and queer theory: Henry Abelove, Michèle Aina Barale and David M. Halperin (eds), *The Lesbian and Gay Studies Reader* (New York: Routledge, 1993), Joseph Bristow, *Sexuality* (London and New York: Routledge, 1997), Annamarie Jagose, *Queer Theory: An Introduction* (New York: New York University Press, 1996), Theo Sandfort, Judith Schuyf, Jan Willem Duyvendak and Jeffrey Weeks (eds), *Lesbian and Gay Studies: An Introductory, Interdisciplinary Approach* (London: Sage Publications, 2000). I would also recommend the following websites which provide accessible introductions to Foucault, Butler and queer theory as well as useful bibliographies and links: www.theory.org.uk and www.queertheory.com
20 John Boswell, *Christianity, Social Tolerance and Homosexuality: Gay People in Western Europe from the Beginning of the Christian Era to the Fourteenth Century* (Chicago: University of Chicago Press, 1980) and *The Marriage of Likeness: Same-Sex Unions in Pre-Modern Europe* (London: HarperCollins, 1994).
21 Michel Foucault, *The History of Sexuality, Volume 1: An Introduction* (New York: Random House, 1978).

22 Alan Bray, *Homosexuality in Renaissance England* (London: Gay Men's Press, 1982).
23 Jeffrey Weeks, *Coming Out: Homosexual Politics in Britain from the Nineteenth Century to the Present* (London: Quartet Books, 1977) and John D'Emilio, *Making Trouble: Essays on Gay History, Politics and the University* (New York: Routledge, 1992).
24 Eve Kosofsky Sedgwick, *Epistemology of the Closet* (Berkeley: University of California Press, 1990).
25 Judith Butler, *Gender Trouble: Feminism and the Subversion of Identity* (London and New York: Routledge, 1990).
26 This is certainly how theologian Robert Goss uses it in his work *Jesus Acted Up: A Gay and Lesbian Manifesto* (San Francisco: HarperSanFrancisco, 1993) and how it is used in Elizabeth Stuart with Andy Braunston, Malcolm Edwards, John McMahon, Tim Morrison, *Religion is a Queer Thing: A Guide to the Christian Faith for Lesbian, Gay, Bisexual and Transgendered People* (London and Herndon, Va.: Cassell, 1997).
27 Ki Namaste, '"Tragic Misreadings": Queer Theory's Erasure of Transgender Subjectivity', in Brett Beemyn and Mickey Eliason (eds), *Queer Studies: A Lesbian, Gay, Bisexual and Transgender Anthology* (New York and London: New York University Press, 1996), pp. 183–203.
28 Susan J. Wolfe and Julia Penelope (eds), *Sexual Practice, Textual Theory: Lesbian Cultural Criticism* (Cambridge: Blackwell, 1993), p. 1.

Chapter 2

Gay is Good

Gay theology began to emerge in the 1970s as gay Christians began to reflect theologically upon the gay liberation movement. In its early days such reflection was dominated by men who felt able to do theology about and on behalf of lesbians but there was some lesbian input and the most prominent lesbian theological voice was that of the American theologian Sally Gearhart who with Bill Johnson edited one of the first books of gay and lesbian theology – *Loving Women, Loving Men: Gay Liberation and the Church*.[1] Johnson was then executive director of the National Taskforce on Gay People in the Church and a minister in the United Church of Christ, Gearhart was an academic who had spent most of her career teaching in Methodist and Lutheran affiliated colleges. Johnson begins his essay 'The Good News of Gay Liberation' by interpreting the Stonewall Riots in Paul Tillich's terms as an assertion of the 'courage to be', 'the ethical act in which a person affirms her/his own being in spite of those elements of her/his existence which conflict with her/his essential self-affirmation'.[2] Gay men and women in finding the courage to be find a hermeneutical lens, the lens of their own experience, with which to observe and expose the patriarchal and heterosexist basis of much Church teaching. This is important not just because gay and lesbian people are marginalised by such teaching but because the close kinship between heterosexuality and patriarchy damages everyone: 'heterosexual relationships and marriage as traditionally experienced are basically unhealthy. They are based on inequality resulting from the male dominance/control mentality'.[3] Gay men offer a different understanding of maleness and of human sexual relationships based on mutuality and equality. Johnson accuses the Church of being over concerned with 'intellectual theology' and under concerned with the grounding of theology in experience. It is therefore vital that gay people come out, articulate their experience and reflect theologically upon it for, 'we who are Gay know the validity of our experience, particularly the experience of our love. That love calls us out of ourselves and enables us to respond to the other. Through our experience of love we experience the presence of God'.[4] This experience must be placed against 'an unexamined tradition that is the source of every form of discrimination we suffer'.[5]

Johnson extends this conflict between tradition and experience to a conflict between faith and law. Faith 'is a profoundly personal, internal affirmation of an unseeable, untouchable truth . . . because we cannot enter into another's life experience, feelings, or encounters with God, we cannot judge the validity of another's affirmation of faith'.[6] It is this personal encounter with God that Jesus proclaimed not a moral law, 'we are Christians, not Paulists'.[7]

Johnson goes on to tackle some of the arguments used against the full inclusion of lesbian and gay people in the life of the Church. He argues that Paul makes it clear that when referring to same-sex relationships he is always expressing merely a personal opinion. Moreover, Paul's teachings on same-sex activity have to be understood against various backgrounds. His cultural background associated such activities with paganism. His theological background was focussed on the imminent return of Christ, and his historical background knew nothing of the concept of sexual orientation. Turning to the view that homosexuality is unnatural Johnson counters that 'the fact that same-sex relationships have been found to exist in every species of animal testifies to the fact that the created order includes homosexuality as a normative form of relating'.[8] Furthermore, heterosexual people themselves have rebelled against the procreative principle in favour of a primarily emotional understanding of sexual activity which, in turn, has led to heterosexual people engaging in sexual activity which previously had been popularly constructed as perverse and unnatural and associated with homosexuality. What both gay and straight people are discovering is that relationship is the essence of the created order.

Johnson adopts a liberationist approach to the issue of sexual ethics drawing a distinction between sexual relationship – 'an integrative, interpersonal, growing experience' which gay people have often been told they are incapable of – and sexual relating in which sexual desire, not love, is expressed. Sexual relating is not sinful as long as it is not exploitative or manipulative and it may well develop into sexual relationship.[9] The Church has traditionally taught that sexual relationship is only possible within marriage, what it has to realise is that marriage is essentially a covenant relationship and that such a relationship is available to people of any gender as lesbian and gay experience verifies. The great fidelity evident in many gay relationships is a 'true' fidelity which has grown from love and freedom not a response to social or religious expectations, it is then a higher form of fidelity than that found in many heterosexual marriages.

The gay liberationist agenda is also evident in Johnson's advocacy of an androgynous/ bisexual understanding of human nature. Indeed this is theologically vital because the divine is itself androgynous and the male dominated Church has failed to comprehend or represent the true nature of God and thereby violates it. He encourages gay people to become aware of their own bisexuality, but such a discovery does not require a rethinking of one's sexual identity, just an awareness of secondary as well as primary feelings.

For Johnson gay liberation is vital for the liberation of the Church to enable it to better incarnate the gospel. This essay ends with a call to all gay men in the Church to come out to ensure that liberation takes place.

Sally Gearhart's essay is on 'The Miracle of Lesbianism'. Gearhart follows the lesbian feminist approach of emphasising the solidarity lesbians and heterosexual women share by virtue of being brought up and living under systems of patriarchy and through an embrace of feminism. She constructs lesbians as women in whom patriarchal conditioning has not completely 'taken', women identified women, not necessarily involved in sexual relationships with other women. This is why a lesbian is a miracle: she holds on to some self-love as a woman. The powers of heteropatriarchy do everything to expunge this self-love and the lesbian has the courage to express this love in the face of thousands of years of condemnation. Gearhart too postulates the bisexual view of human nature suggesting that human beings are socialised into being heterosexual, a socialisation lesbians and gay men resist. It is thus heterosexual people who are really 'unnatural'. The presence of same-sex love in 'every society in every age' testifies to the naturalness of it. Lesbians however choose same-sex relationships over bisexuality for political reasons for in patriarchal society equal relationships between men and women are an impossibility.

Turning to theology, Gearhart argues that an awareness of the degree to which women and women's experiences have been expunged from the Christian tradition forces all women 'to re-evaluate every interpretation of history and every article of our faith'.[10] The Church as an institution is irredeemably patriarchal and therefore incompatible with feminism. Lesbians can only remain within it by developing strong structures of solidarity with other women and coalitions with other marginalised groups. Gearhart also accuses the Church of fostering an 'abstract and heady' theology unrelated to experience in general and women's experience in particular. A lesbian theology then would be 'an absolute and uncompromising denial of what has gone before'.[11] It is a beginning again.

> The 'studying of god' has to come out of experience, has to have base or ground. It cannot come out of abstract conceptualising. Concepts and rational processes will have to wait until we've rediscovered our bodies, our experiences, our histories and our feelings about all these things. Only then can we connect our heads with our experiences as the two have never been connected in Christian tradition.[12]

In 1977 *Towards a Theology of Gay Liberation* was published in Britain edited by Malcolm Macourt, a gay Christian sociologist. In his essay Macourt outlines the gay liberationists' vision of society as one in which young people

> will become aware of a wide variety of life patterns: monogamy – multiple partnerships; partnerships for life – partnerships for a period of mutual growth; same-sex partners – opposite sex partners – both; chastity; living in community – living in small family units ... The goal of the Christian gay liberationists must be that the choice of pattern which *makes most sense* to each and every person will be seen by each most clearly to allow them to accord with the injunctions: 'love the Lord your God with all your heart, with all your soul, with all your mind, and with all your strength' and 'love your neighbour as yourself' (Mark 12.30f.).[13]

Macourt adopts the spectrum/bisexual theory of sexuality which enables people to choose their sexual orientation within the constraints of socialisation. He notes that amongst theologians it is really only evangelicals who are comfortable with the notion of choice in sexual orientation. It is a position which demands much intellectually and theologically. The vast majority of sympathetic ethicists opt for a starting point that lesbian and gay people cannot help their condition.

Jim Cotter, an Anglican priest, takes up the theme of the gay challenge to traditional understandings of human sexuality. Cotter suggests that gay people bring home the reality that to be human is to be a sexual being. Gay people also present the possibility of alternatives to celibacy on the one hand and marriage on the other. It is the quality of a relationship rather than it qualitative length or indeed the level of is exclusivity that matters. Faithfulness is reconstructed so as not equate automatically with monogamy but

> to be 'full of faith', fully of trust, to be willing to let love be vulnerable ... It may be that if I love B deeply, then I am also freed to love C (and both may be sexual loves). For love is not a cake with larger and smaller pieces: only time is the cake which has to be apportioned with care and sensitivity. Love may grow exponentially![14]

Gay people also challenge rigid gender roles. They play the part of the fool or court jester in society telling the truth through unconventional behaviour. In addition they challenge a literalistic interpretation of scripture that does not consider cultural and historical context. They also pose a threat to a static understanding of the natural in natural law. Cotter cites the Roman Catholic theologian Teilhard de Chardin throughout his essay. Teilhard de Chardin believed that creation was in the process of evolution and the act of creation incomplete. In this understanding of the natural order the purpose of sexual organs cannot be fixed for, caught up in the process of evolution/creation, sexual organs are adapting to meet new requirements.

Cotter applies the analogy of eating to sexual ethics. Eating is a fact of life, neither right nor wrong in itself. Though it may be necessary to sometimes eat on your own to fulfil a biological need, it is more satisfying to eat with others. Something is wrong if you eat obsessively or starve yourself, 'but there is a healthy rhythm of fasting and feasting, of abandonment and restraint. There are ultimately, no detailed rules about this …'.[15]

The Roman Catholic theologian Giles Hibbert in his essay argues that from a Christian point of view gay liberation can never be simply a private matter but concerned with the liberation of the whole of society 'such that there is no room, no living space, within it for any form of sexual oppression; and, more positively, that different sexualities can add together within it towards its richness'.[16] A Christian theology of gay liberation must be forged in the white heat of the gay liberation movement not in the abstract environment of academia.

Hibbert starts with assumption that gay liberation has got matters right and Christian tradition has gone wrong. He attributes this erring to a disconnection between moral and dogmatic theology. Thus there has been a separation between the theology of what we do from the theology of what we believe, a split between faith and love, which has produced a hard legalism within the Church. Christians have traditionally also made the mistake of taking the application of the law, for example in Paul's teaching on same-sex love, which is culturally conditioned, as the absolute law which it is not. The absolute law is Christ's new commandment/covenant to love on another (John 13.14). It is only by obeying that law, by loving 'unrestrainedly' that we discover the law for our actual loving. This emphasis on love as they key element in a Christian understanding of human nature is also evident in Norman Pittenger's essay which echoes Cotter's construction of human nature as one that is in process. To be human for Pittenger is to move towards the image of God who is love. Our sexual desire is the fuel that propels us on that road and the fact that a significant minority of people are homosexual demonstrates that for some such desire is the natural route to take. To deny them that path would be to consign them to an inhuman life. Both gay and straight are under the same moral law when it comes to sexual ethics – the command to love and avoid behaviour that is self-seeking and which treats the other as an object –

> I dare not condemn those who engage in promiscuous or easy sexual encounters. But I would say to them that they are *really* wanting something else; they are really seeking for the sort of relationship which has about it the quality of true love … and of the joy which can be found in the widest and fullest sharing of a life with another.[17]

Like Hibbert, Pittenger believes that gay liberation is in fact human liberation, for gay liberation frees human beings from 'irrational, unloving and negative rules', from outmoded traditions and ignorance and prejudice.[18]

The British essays are more gentle in tone than Johnson and Gearhart's but nevertheless some common themes are evident. There is a general adoption of the gay liberationist agenda which does not seek the integration of the gay or lesbian person into pre-existing socio-ethical structures but seeks the radical reform of society and Church to allow for a variety of sexual orientations and expressions. An embracing of the bisexual theory of human nature is also evident in both these volumes. This is, however, combined with a strong sense of gay identity. Gays are presented as people who have clearly defined patterns of relating, they have a distinctive 'experience' which must be placed at the heart of any future theological reflection surrounding sexuality. There is also a tendency to portray the Christian tradition as simply wrong on issues of sexuality and of little use in helping Christians to reconstruct a theo-ethical response to issues arising from sexuality.

It's a Miracle

Early gay theology such as is represented by the two books reviewed above was nothing short of miraculous. What we witness in this theology is a sort of transubstantiation, the taking of a dominant discourse that constructed people with same-sex desire as a species of person, sick, perverse and dangerous, transforming it into something positive. Accepting the designation of themselves as a species, a different type of person because of their sexual desires, these theologians along with other gay liberationists, reversed the discourse claiming that they were therefore in possession of full selfhood, a selfhood that gave them greater authority than the very experts who had 'invented' them to speak about same-sex desire. They therefore dismissed the sick, perverse and dangerous construction and in its place constructed a discourse of gay wisdom. Gay people are presented as being victims of patriarchy and yet managing to create some sort of a vacuum within it, living lives and constructing relationships which manifest qualities of freedom, mutuality, reciprocity and equality – true love – which makes their love in some senses more healthy and more Christ-like than that of heterosexual people.

Gay theologians were able to construct such a discourse because modernity displaced external authority with the authority of the self. Deference to external authority was associated with immaturity, all was to be judged and assessed by the self. This created a sort of democratic environment in which voices previously silenced could make themselves heard by claiming an authentic, autonomous selfhood. What had to be tackled were not the old authorities per se but the exclusive claims to selfhood made or assumed by others, in this case by heterosexuals. Theologically it was crucial for gay theologians to claim gay selfhood because the liberal theology which dominated at the time of these writings located the point of contact between God and humanity in the human self. By focussing on the self liberal theology gave lesbian and gay Christians who claimed full selfhood the tools to think for themselves, to develop theological selves and in the process to expose the heterosexual bias of the dominant discourse. The foundation of early gay and lesbian theology was that gay is good because love is the point of contact between God and the human self. In a context where the selfhood of gay and lesbian people is denied the priority must be self-love because the task must be the creation of an authentic self precisely because in liberal theological discourse the existence of an authentic, autonomous self is a pre-requisite for divine contact. Liberal theology also gave gay theology permission to, if not dismiss, then discount the authority of Christian tradition. The authority of the self displaced all forms of external authority and the historical consciousness of the modern era coupled with a belief in the evolutionary progress of humanity enabled gay theologians to argue that the authors of the Christian tradition simply did not have the tools to understand gay sexuality properly. It also allowed them to construct the debate around sexuality as a debate between hard moral legalism and love/faith, the external versus the internal.

What we therefore encounter in this early gay theology is an ingenious marrying of gay liberationist discourse with liberal theology to establish the selfhood of gay people and therefore their right and ability to do theology, for they have a point of contact with the divine and an experience to reflect upon. Gay people are given a theological voice. Like all forms of liberal theology gay theology is fundamentally apologetic. Though it is in part a rallying cry for gay people, particularly gay Christians, to 'come out' i.e. to acknowledge and proclaim their selfhood, much of early gay theology is aimed at changing the Church. It is impossible to underestimate the importance and brilliance of gay theology and a testimony to its brilliance is the fact that it has not died.

The Theology of John J. McNeill

McNeill was an American Jesuit theologian when he published *The Church and the Homosexual* in 1976.[19] He did not write this book as an openly gay man but it is a scholarly, liberal critique of official Roman Catholic teaching on homosexuality. As a result of the publication of this book McNeill was ordered by the Vatican to refrain from any further public statement on homosexuality and later any ministry to gay or lesbian persons. McNeill attempted to obey for nine years but in the end could no longer square the obedience demanded with his conviction that God had called him to a ministry to gay people. McNeill was expelled from the Jesuits in 1987 at the age of 62. He came out and in 1988 published *Taking a Chance on God* a piece of gay liberal theology.[20]

The theology articulated in *Taking a Chance on God* is founded on two forms of knowledge: psychotherapeutic theory and 'the revelatory experience' of lesbian and gay Christians. McNeill is highly influenced by the nineteenth-century immanentist philosophy of Maurice Blondel. Blondel's influence on McNeill is evident in the latter's emphasis on subjective knowledge, his understanding of freedom as being an essential characteristic of the self, a predominantly immanent construction of the divine presence, an understanding of the human subject as suffering from a privation which only the divine can fulfil and an understanding of truth as the fulfilling of the self's potentiality.

McNeill draws a distinction between mature and immature faith. Immature faith is one which confuses the will of God with that of external authorities and confuses God's voice with that of our own 'sadistic superego' that paralyses us with neurotic guilt. A mature 'healthy' faith is one 'built directly on our own experience, a faith that can lead us to reach out in love to each other'.[21] This faith must be grounded in prayer, in the 'direct and immediate' contact with God that no Church can touch or override. For the Church is prone to preach and incarnate 'pathological' religion, a belief system that fears and punishes freedom of thought. Healthy religion on the other hand enables people to achieve *teleios* (Matthew 5.48), not moral perfection but self-realisation, our full potential.

> We lesbian and gay believers have the right and the duty to carefully scrutinise all religious belief systems and distinguish between those belief systems that support our need to achieve healthly self-acceptance and those that are destructive of our psychic health and maturity.[22]

What McNeill does then is place religion in the dock and place it under the judgement of gay and lesbian experience. He explicitly encourages gay and lesbian people to engage in a process of self-centring as part of the route towards maturity. The Holy Spirit dwells within and the law of the new covenant is written in our hearts – it is inwards that we must go on our search for God. McNeill regards it as no coincidence that lesbian and gay Christian liberation began at roughly the same time as the charismatic movement with the Roman Catholic Church. What the charismatic movement teaches gay and lesbian people is that God can speak to you directly.

For lesbian and gay people finding the self as a 'home' for God involves a jettisoning of the pathological fear, anger, shame, guilt and self-hate encouraged and caused by Church and society. The willingness to let go of the pathological is declared in the process of coming out which is akin to a rebirth, followed by a period of adolescent-like sexual and social experimentation which is in turn followed by a 'settling down' into more stable, committed relationships. As well as being a process of joy and growth this is also a process of mourning, of dying to one's old identity, of letting go of 'normality' in favour of an exiled status in society. It is also a process of learning to trust in God:

> Since we do not choose our sexual orientation, we experience it as given, a part of our created reality. Insofar as our experience of our sexual orientation is negative, as we see ourselves as sinful, sick, or evil, we will experience a deep crisis in our ability to trust the Creator. Only a sadistic God, a God who inspires fear, mistrust, and hatred would do such a thing – not a loving God whom one could address as a loving parent.[23]

Self-love then is the only alternative to belief in a sadistic God.

McNeill then turns to reflection upon what he regards as the special virtues of the lesbian and gay community. These he identifies as hospitality and compassion both of which came into particular prominence in the AIDS crisis. He also presents lesbian and gay people as being gifted celebrants of life. Not in the gay community has the Protestant work ethic stifled the freedom to play. With an exiled status comes a freedom to engage in activity purely for its own sake, for the delight of it. Such freedom comes from a self-love and acceptance and ultimately from an acute awareness of God's unconditional love.

Such self-love must embrace the body and sexuality as gifts of God and McNeill believes it is part of the prophetic mission of lesbian and gay people to lead the Church back to an embracing of embodiment and the sexual as paths to God and to rediscover the playfulness of sex which has been tied to the work ethic of reproduction, even in the Roman Catholic Church, for too long. Playful sex must be between equals who engage in sex in a spirit of mutuality, reciprocity and intimacy. McNeill believes that a committed and faithful relationship is therefore the ideal context for sexual expression but acknowledges that there are many people for whom such a relationship is not possible. All mutually consenting sex is good sex but committed sex is the best.

The sixth part of *Taking a Chance on God* is devoted to AIDS and death and I will examine it in a chapter five. Finally, McNeill turns to the gay Christian community his primary experience of which has been the gay Catholic group Dignity. It is the sacred task of the gay Christian community to give to its members a sense of dignity and to engage in a process of discernment distinguishing between what is 'purely human' i.e. homophobic in the Christian tradition from what is the true word of God. It must learn what it means to love including what it means to love the Church, for McNeill is convinced that lesbian and gay Christians should resist exclusion from their parent denominations. Like any Christian community the gay Christian community has to struggle to divest itself of false idols and the values of the world. But above all the task of the gay Christian community is to discover, reflect upon and proclaim the 'unique gay and lesbian experience of God'.[24]

In 1995 McNeill published a further volume, *Freedom, Glorious Freedom* in which he takes up again the theme of the spiritual journey of lesbians and gay people.[25] This book begins with the statement that a sexual orientation 'is a way of thinking, feeling, and responding that goes to a person's essence. A gay orientation is not something that can be chosen. We are born gay!'.[26] It is therefore necessary for gay people to live out their sexual orientation as best they can. Drawing on Boswell, McNeill suggests that gay people have always been natural spiritual leaders and now God has raised up the lesbian and gay Christian community to change the Church. Once again he argues that such a role is dependent upon gay Christians reaching a spiritual maturity, rejecting pathological religion and trusting in the freedom of their conscience, for it is there, and not in external authorities, that the Holy Spirit dwells. Individually lesbian and gay Christians must learn to 'discern spirits' by listening to their own hearts which is where God is to be found.

In the second part of the book McNeill explores the three stage process of 'creating the authentic gay self'. The first stage in the process is learning self-love through coming out to oneself. This also involves a letting go of a desire to be part of dominant culture and an acceptance of the exile. McNeill suggests that lesbians and gay men should celebrate this stage with a rite very like the sacrament of confirmation. For confirmation is the sacrament of maturity, of recognising the presence of God's spirit within.   The second stage of the process is to move from learning to be intimate with oneself to learning to be intimate with another. Until we know what it is to be loved completely by someone it is very difficult to believe in the unconditional love of God. A great deal of pathological behaviour in the gay community including promiscuity and misdirected anger results from having skipped stage one and launched into stage two. Neither stage can be avoided: 'to know God, you must love. If you never let yourself love with a gay love, you will never (barring a miracle of God's grace) know God intimately in this life!'.[27] The third stage involves being openly gay and Christian and involving oneself in the gay Christian community in order to teach the Church that it is possible to be authentically gay and Christian. One of the ways this may happen is through a public rite of covenanted union. Again, drawing on Boswell McNeill argues that lesbian and gay people are only reclaiming an ancient tradition here, older than that of heterosexual marriage.

McNeill then takes the twelve-step programme developed by Alcoholics Anonymous and attempts to apply its principles to lesbians and gay men. He likes it because it is a spirituality based on personal experience, discernment and autonomy. It is not hierarchical or elitist. The addiction that lesbian and gay people need liberation from is the addiction to the closet, to the values of the heterosexual world and external approval. The first three steps involve acknowledging that we are in trouble and that we are ultimately dependent on God. The journey towards intimacy with God is a journey into the self, to the Spirit that dwells within us. Human beings long for God and only God can ultimately satisfy that longing, all other forms of intimacy are but foretastes of the ultimate intimacy with God. Therefore it is vital to consecrate one's yearning, to be aware of its ultimate *telos* otherwise you will always be tempted to seek fulfilment in that which cannot satisfy.

McNeill does not get beyond the first three steps. He refocuses instead on what he regards as the turning of the ages from one in which the masculine archetype has dominated to one in which the feminine archetype will be predominant. At several points in the previous age however the feminine did push through, for example in the personality of Jesus and in the work of Ignatius Loyola. Eventually the spirit of God will bring together the two archetypes in an androgynous synthesis. But at the moment the gay liberation movement is part of the emergence of the feminine archetype, for gay men represent and are in touch with the feminine within themselves. The gay and lesbian community is a community which can model androgyny – the balance of masculine and feminine in each person – and bonds of friendship and equality. Using Jung McNeill's reflects on the role that gay people play in society including their aesthetic sense, their gifts as teachers, sense of history and, most importantly, their strong spiritual sensibility. The stone that the builders rejected has become the cornerstone of the new age of the feminine.

McNeill is an undoubted and worthy hero of the lesbian and gay Christian liberation movement. His work succeeds in giving gay and lesbian people dignity. Again, it is impossible to underestimate the extraordinary and quite brilliant reversal that McNeill accomplishes in his theology. In the context of the Vatican declaring that the 'particular inclination' of the homosexual person is 'ordered toward an intrinsic moral evil' and the inclination itself 'an objective disorder'.[28] McNeill suggests to gay and lesbian people that not only is their sexuality their route to the divine but they have gifts and virtues associated with their sexual orientation that the Church needs. In the prevailing atmosphere of societal and ecclesiastical homophobia (of which McNeill was a victim) and the emotional and political tolls of the AIDS crisis this was, and indeed still is, good news to the gay community. Furthermore, McNeill directs lesbian and gay readers to a sacred space outside the realm of Vatican authority, a space where it is possible for the lesbian and gay person to hear the voice of God speaking directly to them. This space is their heart/conscience. In going into this space and trusting their experiences lesbian and gay Christians ironically demonstrate themselves to have a faith much more mature and healthy than many of their fellow Christians. In McNeill's theology a despised and beleaguered group of people become the bearers of the gospel to their fellow Christians.

McNeill is able to achieve this extraordinary theological feat because he articulates a classic liberal theological approach (though not in all respects as a chapter five will demonstrate). First McNeill follows the liberal theological path is resting his theology on some epistemological foundations – psychotherapy and the philosophy of Blondel. These constitute the unexamined basis of McNeill's theology. The dependence upon psychotherapy is particularly evident in McNeill's work which is peppered with the language of 'health', 'maturity', 'dependence', 'and addiction'.

Central to McNeill's theology is the gay self. McNeill takes an essentialist view of human sexuality and this is crucial to his argument. One cannot choose to be gay, being gay is part of God's created order, what one can choose to do is to move from an inauthentic selfhood based upon self-hatred to an authentic selfhood grounded in self-love. In typically liberal style this self is constructed as the point of contact between the gay person and God which is why it is vital that it is 'free' to be itself and not bound in an addictive dependence upon external approval. Investing in the authority of the self enables McNeill along with all other liberal theologians to downplay and be suspicious of the authority of external authorities such as scripture, tradition and ecclesiastical hierarchies. Tradition along with all other external authority is placed in the dock under the scrutiny and judgement of experience. The focus on the self necessarily leads to a predominantly immanent construction of the divine.

McNeill represents the later stages of the gay liberationist movement when much of the original radical sexual agenda had been jettisoned in favour of a more reforming approach based upon an ethnic minority model of identity. This ethnic minority model comes out in McNeill's construction of the lesbian and gay community as a community in exile, not quite belonging to the world around them. Nevertheless the exile is necessary in order to preserve identity and the virtues and gifts that accrue to such an identity.

McNeill then employs the theological methods and assumptions of liberal theology and to great effect. Three themes which are prominent in McNeill's work are also evident in other gay liberal theology – coming out as a means of grace, coming out as a form of loss and gay existence as a form of exile.

The Agony and the Ecstasy

At several points McNeill refers to the work of John E. Fortunato. Fortunato, a gay psychotherapist, published *Embracing the Exile: Healing Journeys for Gay Christians* in 1982.[29] In this book Fortunato argues that psychology and spirituality are two dimensions of the same journey, psychology opening the self to the self, spirituality opening the self to the divine. The pre-requisite for spiritual enlightenment is therefore 'a sense of autonomy and self-determination'.[30] In the west, where these two dimensions of life have been severed the result has been the growth of what Fortunato calls 'myth', the humanly constructed metanarratives that explain and order the whole of reality. Gay people are constructed as perverse outsiders in this mythic system. They are exiles in society and like the Israelites in Babylonian captivity this is a place in which they can learn that their previous concepts of God and reality was too small. But this learning experience is painful and is often learnt in the context of psychotherapy. It is painful because it is a process of grief, a process of letting go of the myth and our investment in it. It sometimes involves the letting go of families or at least a partial letting go, it sometimes involves a letting go of a partner and children, of friends. It always involves a letting go of job security, of protection under the law, of the feeling of being secure and safe in your environment including the ecclesiastical environment. It involves letting go of the denial of the reality of oppression, letting go of despair, and letting go of closet. The task of the psychotherapist in all this is to hold a mirror up to the gay patient so that they can see who they really are. The therapist holds up larger and larger mirrors 'until the context is infinity, eternity, the All, God'.[31] For Fortunato Jesus was the divine healer/therapist. He healed people by identifying with them, accepting them as they were and loving them unconditionally. He made people aware of their goodness.

Fortunato's approach is unapologetically psychotherapeutic but his notions of gay exile and grief influenced gay theology enormously. Craig O'Neill, a Roman Catholic priest and Kathleen Ritter, a psychotherapist, developed the loss theory utilising John Schneider's eight-phase model for transforming loss.[32] People involved in this process of losing their life image go through eight stages: initial awareness, holding on (denial), letting go (anger), awareness of loss, gaining perspective, integrating loss, reformulating loss and transforming loss. Like Fortunato O'Neill and Ritter use case studies to illustrate each stage. They then turn to reflection upon the process which they describe as a journey towards 'individuation',

> Individuation is that process through which we journey to the core of our beings, of our selves … The gay and lesbian soul yearns for oneness with the Divine and feels a desire to allow the God of Creation to embrace the God mirrored within. The uniting of the inner and outer experiences of the same God leads toward a wholeness. The self is complete when the lesbian or gay being images her or his core as holy and merged with the divine.[33]

Individuation is evident in an ability to be open rather than rigid, to be more concerned with personal integrity than external authority, to be aware of the interrelatedness of all things rather than suffering from a sense of disconnection, to be creative and compassionate instead of self-centred and to be able to move from the literal towards the symbolic. On this latter point O'Neill and Ritter suggest ways in which gay and lesbian people can demythologise scriptural passages which read literally appear to reinforce heterosexuality:

> The virgin birth may symbolise the opening up of the spiritual possibilities in the gay or lesbian heart where once there may have existed only sterile fear, bitterness, and closeted shame. The imagery and metaphors found in the Song of Songs can be applied to the moral, sexual relationship of two gay men or two lesbians who love each other and can in fact reflect a mystical experience of the Divine. The ascension of Jesus into heaven can come to symbolise a journey not simply into outer space but into inward space, to the place from which lesbian and gay people find their source, the dynamic consciousness within.[34]

O'Neill and Ritter take an essentialist and indeed biological view of sexual orientation – God has created lesbian and gay people and her image is reflected in their souls. The journey that they must take involves letting go of fear and learning to trust in that immanent God.

In works heavily dependent upon psychotherapy the gay and lesbian Christian journey is represented as a journey of the self into itself and therefore into God, a journey which involves mourning the loss of heterosexuality and all it promises. O'Neill and Ritter who offer more direct theological reflection than Fortunato reveal themselves to be classic liberal theologians not only in their focus on the self as the point of contact between God and humanity but also in their demythologising of scripture.

Less heavily dependent on psychotherapy is Chris Glaser, a Presbyterian theologian. Glaser understands the process of coming out as a sacrament, a repeatable sacrament like the Eucharist, for it takes a lifetime to overcome all the impediments to celebrating the gay self. Its sacramental character is evident in the resemblance it bears to the seven sacraments. It is like baptism because it involves dying to an old life and rising to a new one, a life of integrity. It is like reconciliation because we repent of the closet. It resembles confirmation because it affirms 'our creation as gay, lesbian, bisexual and transgendered and ... our citizenship within the commonwealth of God'.[35] Like the anointing of the sick coming out offers a healing and facing of loss. Coming out can be viewed as a form of ministry, a holy order, a witness to the truth and a service to others. Coming out makes authentic relationships possible and so is linked to marriage. But it is to 'communion' that coming out corresponds most closely 'because both involve a sacrifice and an offering that creates at-one-ment or communion with God and with others'.[36]

Glaser suggests that coming out is sacramental because it is related to the nature of the divine and the rhythm of discipleship. The Bible may not mention homosexuality much but it tells many coming out stories. Adam and Eve come out of innocence, God calls them out of their shame at their nakedness. Joseph came out as a dreamer, the exodus was a communal coming out of oppression. Jonathan and David and Ruth and Naomi came out to love, Esther came out of privilege, Jonah came out of anger, Jesus came out of the family, the Samaritan woman came out as herself, Paul came out for grace, the fearful disciples came out of Pentecost empowered. All these acts of coming out involve a letting go of a false reality, a letting go of fear, risk and loss but a coming into truth and integrity. From the Christian point of view God comes out in Jesus Christ, out of the closest of heaven and out of the religious system of his time creating in his wake a community of called-out people, the *ekklesia*. For Glaser it is important to understand that the sacrifice involved in this act was the vulnerability God assumed, not the violence he endured. The violence was not inevitable. To say otherwise is to buy into a scapegoat mentality from which gay and lesbian people have suffered terribly and which Jesus himself resisted. And for Glaser coming out is incomplete until gay and lesbian people serve as Christ to others victimised as scapegoats.

Glaser's hermeneutical strategy of reading the scriptures through the lens of lesbian and gay experience is also evident in the work of Nancy Wilson, a pastor in the Metropolitan Community Church – a Church founded in the USA in 1968 by and for lesbian and gay people. Wilson constructs lesbian and gay identity in terms of a tribal identity.[37] Members of this tribe bear tribal wounds and tribal gifts. Among the tribal gifts are the coming out process, which is a journey into truth and spiritual 'health', same-sex eroticism which challenges heterosexism and patriarchy, humour which holds up a mirror to human folly, 'shamanistic gifts of creativity, originality, art, magic, and theatre',[38] a filling out of the image of God, a pro-life spirituality which cares for children, the earth and stands against violence, an irreverent piety and a spirituality that makes creative use of suffering. 'Promiscuous hospitality' is also a characteristic trait of the queer tribe and thus they incarnate a central biblical ethic. Wilson believes that this tribe has ancestors who appear in the texts of scripture, in the same-sex affection between Jonathan and David, Ruth and Naomi, and the centurion and his servant and particularly in the barren ones and the eunuchs to whom God, through the prophet Isaiah, promises an everlasting name and the assurance that they will 'not be cut off' (Isaiah 56.4–5), a prophecy fulfilled in Jesus' reconstruction of kinship and belonging. The third millennium, which Wilson believes will be the 'queer millennium', promises 'seismic' shifts in out understanding of sexuality. Wilson hopes that we learn to embrace sexuality like Jesus wanted the Sabbath embraced, as a gift to be enjoyed, not over regulated, over which no one should have to die, a gift to remind us of our createdness and the goodness of our creatureliness and relationship with God. It was/is a place of play and refreshment and a place to enjoy equality, 'because sexuality is a universal human experience, one would hope that it could be a bridge, a way in which we could begin to communicate across gender, racial and class lines'.[39] The Church should be a place of Sabbath for lesbian and gay Christians but it is not. In the queer millennium all people will have the right to a Sabbath, and a right 'to be who they are spiritually and sexually'.[40]

Glaser and Wilson are far less dependent upon the foundation of psychotherapy than the other theologians reviewed in this chapter. Nevertheless, it is clear that foundational to their theology is the stable gay/lesbian self whose experience is strong enough to function as a hermeneutical lens through which to interpret scripture and to extend backwards through history in a tribal genealogy. Both sacralise lesbian and gay experience. Like all the theologians examined in this chapter they simply accept the 'fact' that sexuality is the most important 'truth' about a person and the point of contact between that person and the divine therefore to demonise or over-regulate sexuality, gay or straight, is to do violence to that person.

Brilliant but Bankrupt

It is important to stress once again the intellectual brilliance of gay liberal theology. Not only did it reverse a discourse of exclusion and construct one of gay wisdom but like all good liberal theology it reminds us that theology is about real people and affects real lives. All the works mentioned in this chapter are full of stories of real people – moving, horrifying and amusing stories which are deeply engaging. But gay theology has revealed itself to be bankrupt. 'Bankrupt' may sound a harsh description but I choose this word carefully. I do not wish to suggest that gay theology has been a mistake nor do I want to imply that it is completely redundant. Rather, what I want to suggest is that it has proved again and again that it cannot deliver what it has promised. Like all forms of liberal theology gay theology is apologetic – even whilst it may be addressing lesbian and gay Christians and endeavouring to convince them of their spiritual worth, its message is also directed at the wider Christian community. It has failed to produce universally convincing reasons for the acceptance of lesbian and gay people and their relationships within the Church and society as a whole. If

Stonewall can be said to be the creation myth of the gay liberation movement, then the gathering of Anglican bishops at the 1998 Lambeth Conference was apocalypse now for gay liberal theology and its heterosexual advocates. There liberalism demonstrated its inability to withstand pressure from non-western mindsets and the forces of western conservatism combined, its universalism and particularly its advocacy of an essentialist explanation of homosexuality, closing off the possibilities for a more nuanced and pluralistic discussion of same-sex desire that the conference had the potential to inspire.

Nearly 30 years down the line gay liberal theologians have exhausted its possibilities and can only repeat themselves. This is particularly evident in McNeill's work – *Freedom Glorious Freedom* reproduces arguments, stories and whole passages from *Taking a Chance on God* but as the reader will have noted the same arguments that were made in the 1970s were still being made in the 1990s in this body of theology and the same assumptions being made. These include

- the existence of a gay self which needs to move from an inauthentic/pathological existence to an authentic/healthy one, a process that involves grieving for the loss of the privileges that accrue to heterosexuality;
- the self-affirming gay self as the point of contact with the divine;
- the existence of gay wisdom and spiritual gifts which often incarnate gospel values more effectively than heterosexual people and relationships;
- sexuality as essential to human personhood and containing the truth of that personhood;
- the authority of gay experience which exceeds external authority including that of scripture and tradition which can, however, be read through the hermeneutical lens of gay experience.

It is these assumptions and arguments that render gay theology bankrupt, incapable of delivering.

Gay theology has built itself on some very precarious foundations. The gay self is not an incontestable truth. If the social constructionists are right and it was a creation of modernity then it is the creation of heterosexual culture and needs to be not just reclaimed as liberals attempt to do, but scrutinised much more closely, as does the accompanying assumption that sexuality tells the profoundest 'truth' about a person. For all its brilliant reversals, gay liberal theology is still a 'good as you' theology, it still sets heterosexuality as the target to equal and even to beat but never to question. Even those theologians who adopted the bisexual understanding of human nature do not want to jettison the concept of the gay self. Yet the gay self is destined to constantly play theological catch up with the heterosexual self as long as those very categories of sexual identity go unexamined.

Like liberal theology in general gay theology when reflecting upon the gay self assumes a western, middle class self which is magnified into the universal self. This is evident in the descriptions of gay 'spiritual gifts' and is easily falsifiable as indeed is the whole construction of gay 'experience'. It is hard to imagine what McNeill would have to say to a man who claimed that his sexuality was fluid and had changed frequently throughout his life or to non-northern Europeans or Americans who configure sexuality completely differently or Gearhart to a lesbian woman who claimed that it was the Church's telling and enacting of the gospel story that actually enabled her to embrace same-sex desire or any of the theologians to someone who did not think their sexual orientation told the truth about who they were. What could they say except that you are mistaken, suffering from some sort of oppression-illusion and need to be enlightened as to the truth? Like all forms of liberalism gay theology's universalising opens it to charges of colonialism, racism and classism.

Although most of the theologians pay lip service to the vocation to celibacy, they are not terribly convincing. They have followed the path of all western Christian Churches in the twentieth century (including the Roman Catholic Church) in idealising/ idolising sexual desire with the result that the place of the celibate or even the single person is unclear and uncomfortable.

All the theologians surveyed in this chapter have been influenced by feminism, all recognise the link between heterosexism and patriarchy and yet whilst they can see the folly and perniciousness of the 'all women are XYZ' of patriarchal discourse, they imitate it in their own 'all gay people are ABC'. It is just asking for trouble to simply replace the negatives of heterosexist discourse – all gay people are sinful, promiscuous, immature etc – with positives – all gay people are hospitable, spiritually mature, committed to relationships based upon equality and mutuality etc. It is playing the same game as opponents of gay liberation, reducing the gay person to a caricature. Also worrying is the tendency of theologians like McNeill and Johnson to adopt uncritically Jung's theory of masculine and feminine archetypes without stopping to consider the heterosexist and patriarchal foundation of the very concepts of 'masculine' and 'feminine' and the part they play in oppressing lesbian and gay people.

The adoption of the gay self and the crafting of it as the primary point of contact with the divine was undoubtedly necessary within the context of a self-centred dominant theology. I have already made the point that for these theologians such a self provides a refuge from the forces of homophobia. But any theology centred on the self will fall too easily into the trap of identifying God with the self and absorbing the Other into oneself. All too easily the Holy Spirit ceases to be the God of surprises constantly turning the world upside down and forever enlarging our theological horizons, not letting us rest in our complacency and instead becomes the mirror-god simply reflecting our own image. The paraclete becomes the tamed parrot, repeating our own words back to us. Scripture and tradition become authorities to be suspicious of or terrain to be colonised by the gay self rather than possible sites of encounter with a transcendence that lifts us to a different place where we see things from a different angle. This is the irony of the use of psychotherapeutic models for gay liberation for in fact any discourse built upon the self tends towards the neurotic as Lacan pointed out.[41] The self, unable to recognise any authority higher than itself or binding a higher authority too closely to itself is actually in danger of becoming neurotic, of being so turned in itself that it cannot deal with those who are other to itself. There is a danger of creating a hermetically sealed unit of gay Christians unable to engage in genuine dialogue with their fellow Christians who, also living under the tyranny of the modern theological self, are themselves as hermetically sealed. Anyone who has been involved in any form of ecclesiastical 'dialogue' or 'consultation' on the issue of homosexuality will, I think, recognise this scenario of little dialogue and lots of assertion.

Schleiermacher famously claimed that it was the universal feeling of absolute dependence that was the point of contact between humanity and divinity. Gay theologians seem to claim that it is actually a feeling of self worth grounded in one's sexual identity. Everything including God and others are absorbed into the western, middle class, gay and ultimately neurotic self. Early gay theologians used the foundations, principles and tools of modern theology ingeniously to construct the gay theological self the problem is that the gay theological self is hermetically sealed against other selves, it can only speak meaningfully to itself and it is sealed by a modernity that constructed it.

Notes

1   Sally Gearhart and William R. Johnson (eds), *Loving Women/Loving Men: Gay Liberation and the Church* (San Francisco: Glide Publications, 1974).
2   Bill Johnson, 'The Good News of Gay Liberation', in Gearhart and Johnson, *Loving Women/Loving Men*, p. 91.
3   Johnson, 'The Good News of Gay Liberation', p. 94.
4   Johnson, 'The Good News of Gay Liberation', p. 95.
5   Johnson, 'The Good News of Gay Liberation', pp. 96–7.
6   Johnson, 'The Good News of Gay Liberation', pp. 98–9.
7   Johnson, 'The Good News of Gay Liberation', p. 101.
8   Johnson, 'The Good News of Gay Liberation', p. 105.
9   Johnson, 'The Good News of Gay Liberation', p. 108.
10 Sally Gearhart, 'The Miracle of Lesbianism', in Gearhart and Johnson (eds), *Loving Women/Loving Men*, p. 136.
11 Gearhart, 'The Miracle of Lesbianism', p. 142.
12 Gearhart, 'The Miracle of Lesbianism', pp. 142–3.
13 Malcolm Macourt, 'Towards a Theology of Gay Liberation – the Framework for the Debate', in Malcolm Macourt (ed.), *Towards Theology of Gay Liberation* (London: SCM Press, 1977), pp. 24–5.
14 Jim Cotter, 'The Gay Challenge to Traditional Notions of Human Sexuality', in Macourt (ed.), *Towards a Theology of Gay Liberation*, p. 71.
15 Cotter, 'The Gay Challenge to Traditional Notions of Human Sexuality', p. 76.
16 Giles Hibbert, 'Gay Liberation in Relation to Christian Liberation', in Macourt (ed.), *Towards a Theology of Gay Liberation*, p.71.
17 Normal Pittenger, 'What it Means to be Human', in Macourt (ed.), *Towards a Theology of Gay Liberation*, p. 89.
18 Pittenger, 'What it Means to be Human', p. 88.
19 John. J. McNeill, *The Church and the Homosexual* (Kansas City: Sheed, Andrews and McMeel, 1976).
20 John J. McNeill, *Taking a Chance on God: Liberating Theology for Gays, Lesbians, and their Lovers, Families and Friends* (Boston: Beacon Press, 1988).
21 McNeill, *Taking a Chance on God*, p. 8.
22 McNeill, *Taking a Chance on God*, p. 21.
23 McNeill, *Taking a Chance on God*, p. 79.
24 McNeill, *Taking a Chance on God*, p. 201.
25 John J. McNeill, *Freedom, Glorious Freedom; The Spiritual Journey to the Fullness of Life for Gays, Lesbians and Everybody Else* (Boston: Beacon Press, 1995).
26 McNeill, *Freedom, Glorious Freedom*, p. 3.
27 McNeill, *Freedom, Glorious Freedom*, p. 77.

28 Congregation for the Doctrine of the Faith, *Letter to the Bishops of the Catholic Church on the Pastoral Care of Homosexual Persons* (London: Catholic Truth Society, 1986), para. 3.

29 John E. Fortunato, *Embracing the Exile: Healing Journeys for Gay Christians* (San Francisco: Harper and Row, 1982).

30 Fortunato, *Embracing the Exile*, p. 23.

31 Fortunato, *Embracing the Exile*, p. 23.

32 Craig O'Neill and Kathleen Ritter, *Coming Our Within: Stages of Spiritual Awakening for Lesbians and Gay Men* (San Francisco: HarperSanFrancisco, 1992).

33 O'Neill and Ritter, *Coming Our Within*, p. 208.

34 O'Neill and Ritter, *Coming Our Within*, p. 213.

35 Chris Glaser, *Coming Out as Sacrament* (Louisville: Westminster/John Knox Press, 1998), p. 13.

36 Glaser, *Coming Out as Sacrament*, p. 15.

37 Nancy Wilson, *Our Tribe: Queer Folks, God, Jesus and the Bible* (San Francisco: HarperSanFrancisco, 1995).

38 Wilson, *Our Tribe*, p. 51.

39 Wilson, *Our Tribe*, p. 274.

40 Wilson, *Our Tribe*, p. 280.

41 Jacques Lacan, *Speech and Language in Psychosis* (Baltimore: Johns Hopkins University Press, 1981).

Chapter 3

Exodus

In the late 1980s a new strand of theology began to emerge from self-identified gay male theologians. This theology is far less universalistic in its scope and assumptions than gay liberal theology. It is very conscious, for example, of the differences between gay men and lesbians and the experience it grounds itself in is not constructed around the gay self and gay 'gifts' or 'virtues' but the experience of oppression. It also tends to be more critical and interrogating of some aspects of western gay culture and generally takes a social constructionist stance on the issue of identity. Much of it is also obviously influenced by theologies of liberation such as black theology, feminist theology and Latin American liberation theology. This is evident, for example, in the adoption of the methodology of liberation theology often summarised as see, judge, and act. The first stage 'seeing' involves active involvement in and reflection upon the gay liberation movement in order to understand the mechanics of oppression. Judging involves an engagement with the Christian tradition from the perspective of the oppressed and acting involves a return to the gay liberation movement with a strategy informed by the foregoing reflection and so the process begins again. The influence of feminist theology is evident in an acute awareness of the interplay of patriarchy and Christian doctrine and tradition, a consciousness of writing from a male perspective and a refusal to speak for women.

Other influences can also be detected in some of the works in this strand of gay theology of which one is process theology. This branch of theology has also influenced much feminist theology including some lesbian feminist theology. Process theology is panentheistic – God exists in relation to the universe in the same way in which most westerners relate to their bodies, I am my body but also cannot be merely reduced to my body. Process theologians understand the universe to be in process and made up of bi-polar entities which have a physical and mental aspect. One of these entities is God who participates in all that happens in the universe as well as experiencing in himself all that happens. He is therefore a fellow sufferer. As well as having an unchanging essence then God is also always in process like human beings are. Some of the later works in this strand exhibit the influence of radical postmodern theology with its gleeful embrace of the death of God, death of self, death of history and the death of the book and the resultant realisation that all reality is a construct.

In this chapter the work of four gay male theologians will be examined: Michael Clark; Gary David Comstock; Richard Cleaver and Daniel Spencer.

J. Michael Clark

Clark is a freelance scholar and was a founder of the Gay Men's Issues in Religion Consultation of the American Academic of Religion. He has produced a corpus of gay theology beginning with *A Place to Start* which was published in 1989.[1] The key characteristic of this work as far as the author is concerned is that it is 'prophetic' rather than 'apologetic'. Embracing the exile it uses its location at the margins to speak from and to the tradition. Further (and this is to become absolutely central in Clark's approach) such a theology is only concerned with the here and now, pointing to a God not beyond or above but located in the community's experience – the historical experience of an oppressed group of people. Theology is thus horizontal in orientation and anthropological in character, 'our theologising is thus provisional, tentative, dynamic, partial, and never authoritatively complete or "once-and-for-all"'.[2] It makes no claims to be objective and the theologian is conscious of their own subjectivity. But it does seek to change social structures.

The structure of the book follows the liberationist methodology of see, judge and act. Clark begins with an analysis of patriarchy, heterosexism and gay oppression all of which the Christian tradition is deeply implicated in. The result of this absorption and perpetuation of patriarchy and heterosexism has been the creation of what the ancient Hebrews called a *galut*, a community in exile with its own subculture (Clark is obviously indebted to Fortunato's analysis here). This subculture was formed in a situation of oppression and sometimes mirrors the values of the oppressor. But by virtue of its existence this subculture creates a space in which alternative values and different types of relationship can be constructed. Part of the process of self-affirmation is an identifying and rejection of heterosexist values. Clark continues to acknowledge his debt to Fortunato in his conviction that gay people discover God through and in the depths of their grieving for the loss of the promises of the heterosexual world. In that place we discover the God of liberation theology, the God who is on the side of the oppressed and can be encountered among the oppressed.[3] This in itself should induce a feeling of solidarity and compassion for all other oppressed peoples and also give gay people the confidence to risk experimenting with different models of relationship and community.

In the shadow of AIDS a gay liberation theology will also have to wrestle with issues of tragedy and theodicy and with the way in which AIDS has been constructed in western society to 'redouble' the oppression of gay people. AIDS has driven home to the gay theologian the truth of the claim of Latin American liberation theologians that all theology must be a form of praxis. It must be forged in and held accountable to the struggle for survival against the forces of oppression that have constructed AIDS as a gay disease and used it to further justify physical, social and economic violence against the gay community.

Having analysed the forces of oppression Clark moves on to endeavour to 'reconstruct' a theology resistant to those forces. A priority in this process must be the reconceptualising of God, to join feminist theology in the rescuing of the image of God from the limitations of patriarchal and heterosexual constructions. God must be reconceptualised as androgynous or bisexual. The androgyny of God is important to assert to raise human minds above the constructions of gender that delimit male and female behaviour. The bisexuality of God places sexuality at the heart of the divine and rescues sexuality from its association with sin and evil in the Christian tradition. Gay people function as particularly powerful images of such a God in a society still constructed upon the basis of gender and sexual dualisms.

For Clark the tragedy of AIDS requires some rethinking of the nature of God and he draws heavily on post-Holocaust Jewish theologians in this process because they struggle with the same sort of questions as a gay theologian living in the shadow of AIDS, namely how can an all powerful and loving God allow such suffering? Clark constructs an answer drawing upon these Jewish theologians and process theology:

> Perhaps … both creator (God) and creation (creative material) are together from eternity. Since creation is actually portrayed in Genesis as the verbal ordering of chaos rather than as an activity *ex nihilo*, we may even biblically understand that God and chaos are co-eternal. God and creation are one, a yin/yang, two sides of a unitary cosmic coin. Just as creative energy and malleable chaos are one, so the energies for wholeness, beauty, variety, and harmony, and the entropic forces of resistance, fragmentation, and death, are united in a singular, dynamic tension. God and evil are also co-eternal, yin and yang. The cosmic system itself simply exists and is, therefore, morally neutral.[4]

Creation is the evolutionary and never complete ordering of chaos. God and chaos are co-eternal therefore 'things' like AIDS and other types of tragedy will always just happen despite God's will for goodness. The divine/human relationship entails some limits on divine power precisely because it is a relationship – a relationship cannot exist where one party has absolute power. In order then to protect human freedom and to ensure the possibility of a divine/human relationship divine power must be limited to persuasion and God must be capable of being effected by creation. AIDS just happened. God cannot rescue us from it but can suffer with us and is a 'horizontal presence of empowerment for victims of tragedy … God's own anger at tragedy and injustice, and his/her compassion are clearly on the side of the victim'.[5] God is not absent but the force for compassion, rage and political action in our lives. A Christian gay liberation theology must learn from those Jewish theologians who post-Holocaust had to proclaim the death of the pre-Holocaust image of a rescuer-God and return to the ancient Jewish emphasis on ethics rather than eschatology. Vertical theology must be replaced by horizontal theology. A horizontal approach does not construct reality as a mire from which we need to be rescued but a basically good mess that needs to be repaired and tidied. A gay liberation theology must therefore be determinedly this worldly and ethically focussed.

If gay liberation theology must reconstruct the concept of God, it must do the same with Christ. For Clark this involves a radical demythologisation of Christology. He follows the classic liberal view that the historical Jesus was replaced by the mythologised Christ and the feminist view that in the process of divinising Jesus, masculinity and male lordship were also divinised. The process/feminist reconceptualisation of God requires an utterly human Jesus whose significance lies in his embodiment of God's horizontal energy on behalf of the oppressed. This Jesus died himself a victim of injustice. There was no resurrection because there is no 'fix-it' God who can cancel out suffering and tragedy in a flash. What we must proclaim is a suffering God who is present in all human pain and demands our co-involvement.

Clark suggests that eroticising Jesus is a way for gay people to identify with him and make Jesus a powerful symbol of God's presence in the gay struggle. Jesus appears to have had close relationships with men and women and thus is a powerful image of the bisexual God. In his behaviour too Jesus resisted the patriarchal construction of masculinity and therefore also images the androgynous God.

In the third part of the book Clark turns to the practical implications of a gay liberation theology. Clearly, the anthropological and horizontal dimension of such a theology demands action, initially and most importantly in coming out which is an embodied rejection of a heterosexist worldview. In addition, the rejection of a vertical theology in favour of a horizontal one means that gay and lesbian people are themselves aware that their power should also be exercised horizontally. Responsible as we are for our own liberation we must be careful to share and spread around the power we claim. Gay liberation theology must also lead to a reaffirmation of the goodness of the whole spectrum of sexual orientation as a source of knowledge about God and social reality as the twelfth century 'gay' monk, St Aelred of Rievaulx realised. Politically Clark believes that a gay liberation theology will never be happy with mere reform:

> Taking the responsibility, the demand/command, of our gay and lesbian being as an all-encompassing existential standpoint in all its seriousness necessarily moves our theology-as-praxis away from any goal of 'mere' assimilation … . Our ability to create new and genuinely alternative forms – socially, culturally, politically, religiously – requires that we affirm our gay/lesbian difference … .[6]

The gay community is called to be an exodus community, a community leaving behind heterosexism and patriarchy in itself living out right relationship particularly between men and women. It involves resisting all forms of dehumanisation including the dehumanisation of our oppressors. It involves becoming a community characterised by its compassion.

This vision of an exodus community is not a dream for Clark. Such a community is being created and this has been very evident in the community's response to AIDS. The tragedy of AIDS is being redeemed not through some cheap promise of life beyond death but through an assertion of the goodness of sexuality in general and gay sexuality in particular and through a love for the dying expressed in primary care and political struggle:

> The reality of AIDS … unrelentingly fuses theology and praxis. It has compelled gay men (and lesbians as well) toward a deeper self-acceptance and a more realistic acceptance of limitations, both human and divine. It has forced us to wrestle simultaneously with the theological issues of anger and grief and of blaming and forgiveness … Again and again AIDS demands human responsibility for compassionate acts of caring.[7]

Finally, rituals and rites need to be recast in the light of gay liberation theology. The community needs to develop appropriate rites of passage for the process of coming out, hallowing relationships etc. We may also wish to create or recast holidays. Gay men in the USA have already claimed Halloween as their own and in various parts of the world Mardi Gras has also become a focus for the celebration of the gay community. Clark believes that the feast of the Passover is particularly appropriate for gay people to reinterpret and recast for it recalls God's liberation of a particular group of marginalised people. It mixes hope, yearning and defiance. It is a statement of faith in a God who can appear to have forsaken us. It celebrates a God who sides with the powerless. It can therefore be made into a defiant celebration of gay and lesbian sexuality.

Clark took up this theme of 'defiant celebration' a year later in a book of that title in which he focuses on the 'how' of being gay, the ethics that stem from the theological reflection.[8] Clark begins by reprising the key themes of *A Place to Start*. He goes on to argue that the chief obstacle to integrating sexuality and spirituality among gay men is the sexual socialisation of *all* men under patriarchy which encourages a radical divorce of sex from love and a construction of sexual partners as objects which exist for the purpose of gratification. The post-Stonewall cult of masculinity in the western gay community did nothing to alleviate this problem. A theo-ethical praxis must work towards the integration of sexuality and spirituality in gay men and this in itself will impact upon gay sexual practices. Clark wants to explore if and how various sexual practices encourage intimacy, equality, mutuality and compassion among gay men, qualities that can be summed up by the word 'love'. He wants to do this whilst resisting the sex-negative and homophobic discourses of the Judeo-Christian tradition. This, Clark believes, is the specific vocation of lesbian and gay people to free sexuality from its patriarchal and heterosexist constraints and reintegrate it with spirituality.

Clark first turns his attention to the issue of monogamy. He argues that the ideal of monogamy is imposed upon western society as part of the package of heterosexist, patriarchal sexual ethics. Lesbians and gay men cannot simply accept it as ethical truth despite the pressures put upon them to do so by dominant ethical discourses that emerged with AIDS. As people who exist at least partially outside the structures of procreative sex and the nuclear family and as people acutely aware of the differences between 'safe' and 'unsafe' sex lesbians and gay men bear 'both the freedom and the burden of choice' regarding the construction of sexual relationships.[9] No consensus exists in the gay and lesbian community about which is preferable, an open or closed relationship. So Clark considers the ethical advantages and disadvantages of both.

Non-monogamy whilst providing an alternative to the possessiveness implied in heterosexual models of relating may in fact encourage the objectification of sexual partners that patriarchy breeds in men. Jealousy, envy and low self-esteem can manifest themselves in monogamous and non-monogamous relationships. These are the real 'problems' in any relationship and are expressions of our own insecurities. Only by loving ourselves first, by being assured of our own self-worth will any relationship work and this is what western society has worked to deprive gay men and lesbians of. Intimacy is only possible when these things have been defeated.

Monogamy, on the other hand, may create the stability needed for intimacy to develop between two people but its structure may also simply disguise a failing or failed relationship in which intimacy has died or is dying. Clark therefore seeks for guidelines to follow in all relationships – is the relationship just, mutually empowering, is the relationship life-giving to both parties, does it enhance the dignity of all involved, does it move both partners towards wholeness? Relationships must be faithful but Clark wants to redefine the concept of fidelity so that it does not relate primarily to sexual exclusiveness but to the whole relationship – are partners faithful to the relationship they have constructed and negotiated? This type of fidelity requires enormous emotional openness between partners and deep levels of communication, nothing can be assumed. This is the hard work of intimacy, the work of friendship.

Clark finds it significant that sociological research has revealed that gay men and lesbians do not define their primary relationship in heterosexual terms e.g. as 'marriages' but rather, understand themselves as 'best friends'. A friendship model seems to encourage mutuality and equality, autonomy and non-possessiveness. Clark argues that theologically there are ample precedents for valuing same-sex friendship as a route to divine love. Aelred of Rievaulx taught that male friendship transformed the soul lifting it from carnality and enabling it to ascend to the spiritual. Jesus himself had enjoyed such love 'a heavenly marriage' with the Beloved Disciple and it itself was a reflection of the love between God and his Son which provides the pattern for all friendship. Aelred was a monk writing to and for monks and hence sex-negative in his theology but Clark believes that contemporary gay people can take his theology and integrate it into a sex-positive approach:

> Aelred's progression must be conflated and both the love of God and a responsible sexual love rightly ordered. Irresponsible or dehumanising or impersonal promiscuity is precluded, while a responsible gay orientation is still affirmed. Sexual love, gay or non-gay, should simply facilitate rather than circumvent or distract from communion with the divine in the encounter with another person.[10]

Within the Hebrew scriptures David and Jonathan and Ruth and Naomi also provide classic models of same-sex friendship and reprising his bisexual construction of Jesus, Clark notes that Jesus' relationships with both men and women appear to have been built upon friendship.

Clark then turns to reflect upon the ethics of 'radical sexuality' i.e. leathersex and sadomasochism around which there is considerable ambivalence within the lesbian and gay community. Some argue that the whole culture of these sub-communities reinforces patriarchal values and constructions of sexuality in terms of domination/submission and may also involve an acting out of internalised homophobia in the pain and punishment that sexual partners inflict upon one another. On the other hand it is possible to read these sub-communities as subversively playing with notions of gender (particularly masculinity) and domination. Furthermore the sexual activities involved refocus pleasure away from the genitals alone and radically construct sexual activity as a form of play which is capable of a spiritual dimension, participants often experiencing some sense of transcendence at their physical limits. Such activities often involve profound levels of trust, vulnerability and communication and Clark thinks that it is no accident that it is members of this sub-community who have often been at the forefront of AIDS support, their sexual activities having engendered within them deep levels of compassion and sensitivity.

Clark concludes that a sexual ethic built around friendship allows gay and lesbian people the greatest possible freedom in the construction of their sexual relationships whilst providing a theo-ethical framework with which to interrogate our lives and relationships.

Clark's reflection on theo-ethics is broadened in his next book which attempts to put gay theology in ecological perspective.[11] The gay urban ghetto whilst providing a safe space for gay people can also restrict our vision. If gay liberation should produce a compassionate people with a sense of solidarity with all the oppressed, the oppressed must include the earth. This involves re-evaluating the home and the 'private' sphere as the place where politics, particularly eco-politics begins. The other side of this coin is the realisation that gay people have been treated like so much of the earth as of no value and disposable. In the dualistic structures of hetero-patriarchy gay people have joined women and nature on the 'bad' side. Like other minority groups their ghettos are often to be found in ecological waste lands.

In this book Clark is far less grounded in the Judeo-Christian tradition. He characterises it as a religion of 'the power-holding status quo ... including industrialisation (and its imperialistic exploitation of peoples and nature) and the objectification of scientific endeavour (and its devaluation of matter and, thence, nature)[12] against which the prophetic minority has been largely unsuccessful. Christianity by constructing God as separate from the world and by advancing a transcendent, eschatological spirituality has devalued the earth. By valuing the redeemed whole classes of people have been dismissed as of no intrinsic value. It is not solely to blame for the ecological crisis but it shoulders a great deal of blame.

In seeking an appropriately ecological spirituality Clark seeks to construct a spirituality in which dualisms are collapsed and re-centred on 'a radically horizontal god/ess-with-us … immanent or incarnate in everything, throughout all life in both biosphere and geosphere. Ultimately matter and spirit are one; all is sacred'.[13] Because s/he is utterly immanent the divine demands we take care of one another and the earth of which s/he and us are a part. The eco-feminist construction of the earth as God's body resonates with gay liberation theology which has fought for the revaluing of the body but forces gay people to look beyond human bodies to the valuing of all forms of embodiment which are interdependent and interconnected.

Clark revises certain key theological and social concepts from a gay ecological perspective. Sin he redefines as anthropomorphism, the disregard for any other being, acting as if humans owned creation and are not interdependent with the whole eco-system. A certain type of judgement is contained in natural disasters caused by human neglect or violence but it is not divine judgement. Such 'blaming the victim' will always be unacceptable to gay people who have lived through the AIDS crisis and experienced the violent effects of such a discourse. Justice must now be understood as right relation which includes right relation with the earth. All forms of life are intrinsically valuable and though humans may need to kill to live they are obliged to do so only out of necessity and with due respect for the life being taken.

Gay people already represent diversity, otherness and non-productive sexuality in a society which devalues these things. Clark calls upon gay people to recognise their closeness to a devalued earth and to begin to live in harmony with it.

The tone of Clark's 1997 book *Defying the Darkness* is markedly different to that of his previous books.[14] It is written out of the violence of homophobia in North American culture, the terror of living with HIV and a certain lack of satisfaction with his own previous attempts to reflect theologically upon the meaning of this experience. It tends towards a radical postmodern nihilism. It is also written out of an embracing of 'queer' transgressive action, but not queer theory. In the stark reality of AIDS this means affirming life in the midst of death, to reflect ethically upon that life i.e. to plan for the 'long haul' and to confront issues of theodicy. Furthermore this reflection has to be done on some very shaky theological ground. For Clark finds that as a gay man living in this context the only thing he can give authority to is the experience of living life at the margins – scripture, tradition and institutions can have no authority for him because they are implicated in hetero-patriarchy and in the ecological crisis. Once again, but even more strongly, he identifies eschatological thought as dangerous and death-dealing to the earth and to marginalized people upon it. Apocalyptic hope is an expression of despair, an expression of failure. However, engagement with fellow gay theologian Ron Long over the issue of AIDS and theodicy made Clark review his commitment to a process theology. For Long, a process theological approach assumes that God 'tolerates' AIDS at the very least and at it suggests that God is actually involved in the co-creation of the virus and this is an obscene idea. For Long process theology lets God off the hook and discourages anger towards the divine. Long's critique coupled with a growing awareness of his own mortality (Clark was diagnosed HIV+ in 1990) and that of others forced Clark to back track from his plunge into ethics and revisit the whole issue of theodicy.

Clark wishes to revise his process understanding of the divine in order to include the possibility that God is not all good, there is darkness in God, which is not to say that God is capricious or abusive but simply to say that life and death, celebration and suffering are part of the same web of life. This is the realisation of Job of course and just as justice is not vertically given so is tragedy and evil horizontally created. This forces Clark to take a very different view of AIDS than he had done previously. It means facing the fact that though it may have 'just happened', gay men might have contributed towards exposing themselves and others to it:

> Tragically, HIV/AIDS becomes a powerful sign (albeit not the only one) of the extent to which we gay men have been willing to wound one another with our phallic weapons – from protesting bathhouse closings a decade ago, to advocating multiple sexual encounters as the monolithic qualifier of liberated gay identity, to failing to support what too often become undervalued and consequently broken relationships.[15]

The only way out is to take responsibility for our own lives, to live as if God does not exist. And whilst Clark continues to assert the ethical priorities must be mutuality, equality, diversity, compassion, self-criticism and eco-friendly praxis he is now much more circumspect in his ethical judgements. He is more sceptical of the ability of non-monogamous relationships to realise these ethical ideals and he is far less idealistic in his treatment of leathersex/sm.[16] For Clark gay ethical ideals are important because they are statements of defiance against the darkness and even against a God implicated in suffering.

In Clark we encounter a gay male theologian who sets out to avoid the weaknesses of liberal theology whilst speaking from the communal experience of oppression. He is careful to draw on lesbian feminist theology as well as other gay theology in his attempt to articulate that experience of 'hurt' and to reflect on how to exodus from it. He demonstrates the great strength of liberationist theology – the grounding of theology in 'otherness' in the oppression of those excluded from dominant theological discourses and the importance of bringing their experience of oppression into dialogue with the tradition. But the weaknesses of Clark's theology are obvious ones. He goes further than most Latin American liberation theologians in arguing that only a process God can 'speak' to lesbian and gay experience. The problem with a process God is that s/he ultimately disappears and being of no help the point of worshipping such a god or indeed doing theology becomes increasingly difficult to comprehend. So horizontal does God become in the radical postmodern approach that s/he becomes virtually identified with the experience of the oppressed and so theology is collapsed into ethics, anthropology and cultural studies and this process is evident in Clark's corpus of work. The result is a certain hopelessness, for the oppressed are dependent entirely on their own defiance. This is probably meaningful for gay people who have the economic and social resources to be defiant but not all do. It is hard to work out on the basis of Clark's anti-transcendent theology why the gay or lesbian person has a better case than the homophobe and why might should not in the end make right. If God cannot be the guarantor of justice for the oppressed and for the value of equality, mutuality and reciprocity over inequality and oppression then it is hard to motivate oneself for the long haul of social, religious and political struggle. Also without a transcendent referent it is hard to maintain a self-critical edge to one's praxis. If AIDS did nothing else it exposed how helpless and vulnerable we ultimately are and how easily the fruits of a political struggle are plucked and thrown away. It could be argued that AIDS exposed the futility of human self-confidence and defiance – the very things that Clark believes that we must reply upon.

Exodus and Resurrection: Comstock and Cleaver

Gary David Comstock who is a minister in the United Church of Christ and an academic theologian also wants to construct a resolutely unapologetic gay theology whilst recognising the impossibility of basing such a theology on universal categories.[17] Although he states quite categorically that 'Christian Scripture and tradition are not authorities from which I seek approval; rather, they are resources from which I seek guidance and learn lessons ...'.[18] he is, nevertheless, much more deeply rooted in those resources than Clark. Comstock argues that the Christian faith is constructed around two events, the exodus and the resurrection. These events constitute the 'ethical norms by which we live as Christians'.[19] They are events about the transforming of pain. Christians are people, then, who do not bear pain but transform it. These are the two defining events of Christianity and the norms by which all other Christian material and praxis including other scripture is judged. What these two events teach us is that the Christian life is about building community in which all voices, particularly those of the disempowered and oppressed are valued.

Comstock approaches the Bible as a friend rather than a parent,

> as one to whom I have made a commitment and in whom I have invested dearly, but with whom I insist on a mutual exchange of critique, encouragement, support, and challenge ... Although its homophobic statements sting and condemn me, I counter that those statements are themselves condemned by its own Exodus and Jesus events. Just as I have said to my friends, 'How can you express love and be a justice-seeking person and not work to overcome the oppression of lesbians and gay men?' in my dialogue with the Bible I ask, 'How can you be based on two events that are about transforming pain, suffering, and death into life, liberation, and healing, and yet call for the misery and death of lesbians and gay men?'[20]

Lesbians and gay men must not seek to excuse or contextualise away passages like Leviticus 18.22, 20.13 or Romans 1.18–32. They are vicious and misleading in their descriptions of lesbian and gay people and they continue to underpin and bolster homophobic violence. What we can do is learn how not to be community from Leviticus and how not to react when we as a community we find ourselves under threat.

Comstock does not think it helpful to take comfort from Jesus' lack of teaching on the subject of homosexuality. His own experiences of growing up in which he knew his sexual orientation even though he did not have a culture or name for it makes him believe that there have always been gay people and that there were some in Galilee. But it is right for lesbians and gay men to isolate countertrends in scripture, an alternative voice to the patriarchal one that dominates. This alternative voice can be heard in the Song of Songs where the male and female lovers are presented as equals and sexuality is celebrated without any reference to procreation. It can also be encountered in the covenanted love between David and Jonathan. The one role model that Comstock has been able to identify within the Bible is Queen Vashti in the Book of Esther. Vashti is the disobedient queen who defies convention and causes a crisis in the patriarchal order. Her story is not designed to elicit our sympathy but rather prepare the way for the virtuous Esther but gay people can read her story as good news,

> In lifting up her little-known or ignored story – in bringing it in from the margin to the centre – in rewriting her story in our actions today, we use the Bible as a resource for moral agency, for making things better, for making justice.[21]

Comstock believes that God is not confined to the pages of the Bible – he names as sacred Scripture literature which affirms his sexual orientation, modern novels, Native-American narratives and so on. His 'tradition' is the lives of gay men and lesbians down the ages preserved in autobiography, letters etc. These are lives that give him strength, that give him a sense of identity. And the experience he draws upon is his own, his deepest cravings, his experience of the erotic, his deep, non-rational knowledge, the knowledge, his body-knowledge that told him he was gay before he ever heard the term.

There is much in Jesus' ministry that challenged the patriarchal structures of his day but his ministry was not complete, it still needs completing and from him we can take encouragement to break, change and repeal laws that do not allow life to flourish. Comstock is uncomfortable with the political practice of 'using Jesus as our trump card', using Jesus to bolster arguments or praxis because all Christians can and do this with the most powerful group securing ownership of Jesus' image. Jesus did not want to be our master but our friend,

> Quite remarkably, it is Jesus as the master who says, 'Don't look to me for answers, you're on your own. If you want my advice, and it's the last I'm going to give you, it's that you work things out with each other. Look to each other; don't look to me. I'm not the boss, simply a friend who's soon dead and gone. Good-bye' ... . The example does not offer up yet another master; it shatters the master-slave relationship into one of friendship, and not a sentimental friendship of holding on and dependence, but a friendship of challenge, letting go, and affirming independence.[22]

Jesus therefore nudged people to get on without him. The resurrection was not a literal raising of the actual body of Jesus or even a remembering of Jesus so that he lives forever, but a taking responsibility for our own lives in the confidence that nothing can stop the movement to liberation and freedom.

In the light of this radical decentering of Jesus Comstock has to rethink the notion of salvation. In the lives of lesbians and gay men the Stonewall Riots of 1969 are their exodus story and experience, their grasping of freedom, their 'no' to oppression which like the exodus must be relived and re-enacted every day as they struggle in the wilderness.

Salvation is the active protestation against inequality and the catching up of others in that process. Comstock also recasts the Trinity. For him God is the creative power of mutuality and reciprocity in relationships. God is found in relationships, in the love that exists between people (this is what the story of David and Jonathan teaches, God does not broker their covenant, he is not party to it, he rather *is* their covenant. Similarly God is only present in the love between the man and the woman in the Song of Songs). Sin is the violation of mutuality and reciprocity. Jesus is our friend, he saved others by befriending them and receiving their friendship as if lives depended on it. The Spirit is the community that encourages each and every person to share their gifts – it is the power of inclusive community.

Richard Cleaver writing from a Roman Catholic background adopts methodologies and themes similar to Comstock's whilst at the same time constructing a rather different theology. Cleaver explicitly adopts a Latin American liberation theology methodology in his attempt to construct a gay liberation theology.[23] Like Comstock Cleaver focuses on the two events of exodus and resurrection as paradigmatic theological moments in the scriptures. For Cleaver, however, the significance of these events lies in the fact that they reveal the divine as one who saves through the creation of new types of peoples. Unlike Comstock Cleaver is a social constructionist . He understands the Stonewall Riots in terms of the creation of a new people who rejected the labels and identities constructed for them by others. And therefore he believes that lesbian and gay people would be better placed looking in scripture for stories of people breaking out 'of the slavery of social and personal relations patterned by gender or class or race' rather than speculating about the desire of David and Jonathan. The story of the exodus is such a story and there are lessons to be learnt from it. One such lesson is to avoid the temptation of thinking that one can take short cuts to liberation by creating a mirror image of 'Egypt' or by trying to buy our way out through the creation of 'neighbourhoods' and a consumer based culture. The Stonewall Riots of 1969 were the Passover of lesbian and gay people – the symbolic moment at which a group of people turned their back on oppression and claimed a shared history. They are like the Church, a people 'called out' of the mass of humanity to be different, to be a different type of men and women and to live community differently. Having come out we now wander around like the Israelites in the wilderness learning how to become a people, naming ourselves, learning to speak with our own voices, claiming a collective history and developing a class consciousness.

Cleaver's chief theological point is that salvation is never an individual matter, it is found in political action, by acting in solidarity with others, by rejecting the values of 'bourgeois religion' in favour of the establishment of a new type of 'family'. The rejection of the idol of 'family' is one of the clearest messages of the gospel. What the exodus and the resurrection created was a ragbag group of slaves and social misfits and in both cases a purity system eventually corrupted the memory of the origins of the communities. Lesbian and gay people must resist the temptation to respectability and bourgeois values. There is no getting around or out of the category of homosexual anymore than the concepts of 'Samaritan' or 'publican' could have been abolished in New Testament times but one can live that category subversively to expose and question its purpose. One way of doing that is by building solidarity through liturgy and ritual, through a sense of embodiment and through a fearless formation of friendships. This is the completion of Christ's resurrection in community, the creation of a community of lovers out of a lover who gave his body to be touched and to touch, to eat and to be eaten, to die but to be never separated from his friends. Jesus is known through liturgy, through the ritual of the Eucharist and other sacraments. This is what the Catholic Church has always taught and the irony is that it is largely dependent (in the west at least) on gay men to keep the liturgy going. They are the priests, the bishops, the servers, the singers and the readers. Because they have been forced to have a greater sense of embodiment by the societal construction of homosexuality they have been the ones to embody Christ for the Church. The liturgical epistemology and praxis of gay men is evident in the rituals developed around AIDS, in the annual celebration of the Stonewall Riots, in the claiming of Halloween and Mardi Gras and Cleaver believes that more must be done because liturgy is a way of embodying the vastness of our love and scripture teaches again and again it is through great love, love that reaches wider and embraces more than would ever be thought respectable, that outcasts are redeemed.

In Comstock and Cleaver we encounter gay theologians much more deeply engaged with the Christian tradition than Clark. They both regard the exodus and resurrection as paradigmatic events but when they bring these events to bear upon the experience of lesbian and gay oppression very different theologies emerge. For Comstock these events point beyond themselves, they force lesbian and gay people to stand on their own feet, to experience God in the mutuality of their relationships and the inclusivity of their community rather than rely on Jesus, scripture and/or tradition to save them. Cleaver is far less of a demythologiser than Comstock. He sees a family resemblance between the creation of the new classes of peoples out of the exodus and resurrection and the creation of lesbian and gay identity post Stonewall. What is revealed in the biblical events is the fact that God saves primarily through the creation of new classes of people who model humanity and love differently.

Gay and Gaia: Daniel T. Spencer

In the work of Daniel Spencer we come upon a gay male theologian who is attempting to systematise the methodologies and reflections of gay male theology and lesbian theology and critically appropriate them for the purpose of producing 'a liberationist ecological ethic that takes seriously lesbian and gay male experiences and insights'.[24] For, like Clark (whose influence he acknowledges) Spencer is convinced that the erotic and the ecological are fundamentally connected which is why the same people who oppose the extension of human and civil rights to lesbian and gay people are often the same people who oppose all efforts to protect the environment. Both the erotic and the ecological are about a sense of interconnectedness, a proper sense and celebration of one leads to a proper sense and celebration of the other. Spencer draws heavily on eco-feminist theology particularly the imaging of the earth as God's body articulated by Sallie McFague[25] but marries it with the liberationist notion of the epistemological privilege of the oppressed, particularly lesbian and gay people, in order to explore what insights lesbian and gay theology might make to an ecological ethic bearing in mind that lesbian and gay sexualities have been constructed as 'unnatural' and outside human and natural ecologies. In this task he follows Clark and Comstock in viewing scripture as a resource rather than a rule-book in the process of ecological liberation and understanding authority as residing in the communitarian values of right-relation. Spencer adopts a social constructionist approach to sexual identity and indeed to all forms of knowledge. So, for example, he utilises Bernadette Brooten's social constructionist analysis of Paul's construction of human nature noting that sexuality is always about power and particularly the power of men over women and in Roman culture sexuality was constructed around notions of active (associated with maleness) and passive (associated with femaleness).[26] An awareness of the social construction of human nature is important for creating the possibility of different constructions in the future which will allow for a greater ecological awareness to be built into the notion of being human.

Spencer takes up the valorisation of friendship in gay and lesbian theology arguing that as well as providing an alternative relational foundation to heterosexual marriage which includes lesbian and gay relationship, it is also deeply ecological,

> Whilst friendship includes both joy and loss, nothing is ever wasted or lost. Each experience of friendship is recycled into new experiences, adding a strand to the fabric of our friendship histories that give meaning and continuity to our lives. Friendship provides an ethical grounding of actively befriending creation as our normative stance.[27]

He also absorbs the identification of the divine with the erotic, a key element of lesbian theology which will be examined in the next chapter. The gay and lesbian focus on the quality of mutuality in relationship is an important one from an ecological perspective because it 'pays attention to differences in power [and] acknowledges the distinctive nature of human agency while drawing attention to the reality of subjectivity in other creatures'.[28] The construction of the divine image in contemporary theology must foster both the liberation of lesbian and gay people and of the earth and the images employed by gay and lesbian theology do just that – friend, lover, right relationship. Spencer also agrees with Clark that any ecological ethics must centre upon a God who is limited, a God who is a co-sufferer and empowering companion but 'does not violate the ecological parameters of the earth as a living system or intervene to rescue us from the destructive consequences of our actions'.[29]

Much of Spencer's book is devoted to critical analysis of other eco-theologies. He finds a biblically based stewardship theology to be far too uncritically rooted in the patriarchal notions of mastery, ownership and hierarchy that underpin most biblical texts. Liberal theological approaches work with existing structures of power and universalise particular experiences particularly those of white, western, heterosexual men. Process theology is more promising but it too tends to speak with an overarching, universalising voice rather than recognising the difference that oppression makes. Furthermore the process approach dissolves the prophetic, God works solely through persuasion like a typical middle-class gentlemen but such an approach is inadequate in the fact of crisis and oppression. The ecofeminist approach is the most acceptable one to Spencer for in the work of someone like Rosemary Radford Ruether[30] Spencer finds a theologian who is prepared to acknowledge that nature and culture are socially constructed, that the voices of God and Gaia are only heard through the mouths of human experience. She constructs the divine as the matrix of life. Unlike liberal theologians she earths redemption in the here and now and rejects an eschatological theology. Unlike process theologians she recognises the need to incorporate a liberationist dimension into an eco-theology. But Ruether does not address issues of heterosexism or the connection between lesbian and gay oppression and devaluation of the earth. Spencer also criticises Ruether for marginalizing Christology in her theology. He argues that unless the majority of Christians can be convinced that the love of Gaia is related to the love of Christ eco-theology does not have a hope of permeating Christian consciousness.

Finally Spencer outlines a gay ecological theology. Whilst a high degree of mobility and displacement characterise western gay life and may lead to a sense of ecological alienation, in their determination to find one another and build community and in their reclamation of pleasure and beauty gay and lesbian people demonstrate ecological values which they need to consciously acknowledge and develop. Particularly in their embracing of the erotic lesbians and gay men develop a sense of interconnection and friendship which extends beyond themselves and beyond the human. Spencer critiques Clark's fear of hierarchialisation that leads him to argue for the absolute and equal value of all life whilst ultimately fashioning an ethic that prioritises the human over the animal.

Spencer prefers a graded understanding of intrinsic value which becomes part, but only part, of any ethical analysis of a conflict between human and non-human life. Spencer believes that lesbians and gay men have much to learn from Native American ecological wisdom and its connections to spirituality and sexuality. He believes that Native American respect for ambiguity and diversity, including sexual diversity, evident in the existence and valuing of the *berdache*, (a physically male person who nearly always related sexually to other men and undertook work normally reserved for women, the *berdache* was believed to have been endowed with enormous spiritual power) is a result of their respect for nature. Christian missions destroyed the *berdache* tradition.

Features of an 'erotic ethic of ecojustice' will include an appreciation of and attention to embodiment and a resistance to a dualistic split between spirit and matter which the doctrine of the incarnation should in any case make impossible, a valuing of lesbian and gay experience and the diversity within it, a refusal to buy into western society's idolisation of disposability, dispensability and exploitation which has impacted negatively upon gay people particularly in the age of AIDS and a commitment to applying an ethic of gay and Gaia in the lesbian and gay communities. This latter point will include a critique of its consumerism (as Cleaver noted for different reasons), a rethinking of the limits of sexual relationships to ensure that viruses and parasites are not spread between our bodies, and a rethinking of our relationships with animals particularly in what we eat and what we wear. For all his ecological awareness Clark did not consider the ecological ethics of the place of leather in gay eroticism.

Gay Theology and the Disappearance of Theology

Gay liberation theologies are effective in acknowledging and dealing with the otherness of gay sexual identity and its social construction. They locate the divine not in the problematic modern self but in the between-ness of persons and much more effectively than liberal theology they expose the heterosexism and homophobia at the heart of dominant theological reflection and suggest strategies to deal with it. They resist the universalising tendencies of liberal theology whilst trying to reflect upon the theo-ethical implications of the pain of oppression experienced by lesbians and gay men. But there are still weaknesses in this approach. The first is the issue of identity. Most gay liberation theologians take a social constructionist approach to sexual identity but then they leave the issue alone and continue to work with the concept of gay/ lesbian identity leaving it largely unexamined. Cleaver suggests that gay and lesbian people will emerge from the wilderness as a class, a class built around sexual identity. The very language of liberation also reinforces this sense that what is needed is freedom to be, the 'be' being already determined. So the fact that the modern homosexual identity is the creation of forces which sought to suppress same-sex desire by pathologising it is acknowledged but not reflected upon. Gay liberation theology advocates a standpoint epistemology, a sort of Gnosticism, a metaphysics of substance even whilst most of it claims to accept a social constructionist approach. Theologians in this tradition implicitly make an identification between sexuality and truth, not only is it a gay or lesbian person's sexual orientation that leads them out, into exodus, but it is the experience of being oppressed on the grounds of sexual orientation that provides the hermeneutical basis from which the Christian tradition is assessed. But a radical social constructionist perspective can never allow such an identification. What these theologies offer in the end is salvation through homosexuality and it is questionable whether that is any more attractive or theologically sound than salvation through heterosexuality which is what modern theology has tended to posit. It also assumes that, though it may be socially constructed, homosexuality is still stable enough a basis upon which to be saved.

Connected to this is the sharp dichotomy drawn between oppressors and the oppressed in gay liberation theology, a distinction which does not bear much scrutiny. The Church, as Cleaver acknowledges, is packed with gay people. Many, particularly gay men, hold positions of power in the Church. Gay people are among the oppressors as well as the oppressed. It is not enough simply to say that the problem is with the closeted because most gay people have been closeted at some point in their lives and most remain closeted in some aspects of their lives. Gay people exist among the oppressors. Gay liberation theology fails to deal with this reality and in the process fails to deal with the gay nature of the Church, the part the Church has played both in constructing and demonising the sodomite/modern homosexual through its discourses and, perhaps even more importantly, the part the Church has played in producing same-sex desire. For even whilst the western Church was creating and condemning the category of sodomite and even whilst the modern Roman Catholic Church, for example, has uncritically bought into the notion that there are such things as 'homosexual persons' whose sexual orientation is objectivity disordered, it has been manufacturing the desire it condemns. As Richard Rambuss has noted, Catholicism, by centralising within its devotional matrix the semi-naked male body of Christ, has actually induced homoerotic desire in a manner for which it now refuses to take responsibility.[31] This is brought out brilliantly in Antonia Bird's 1995 film, *Priest*, where Fr Greg confesses, concerning his struggle with his homosexuality, 'I sit in my room sweating. I turn to him for help. I see a naked man, utterly desirable. I turn to him for help, and he just makes it worse'. This utterly desirable Christ is the object of homoerotic devotion in art and literature across the Christian centuries. Rambuss focuses on the manifestation of this devotion in the metaphysical poets, some of whose work lurks at the back of the *Divine Office*, including Donne's *Holy Sonnets* which pleads for the "three personed God" to "batter my heart" and "ravish me".[32] It is, however, traceable throughout Christian history. Although overwhelmingly male, there are also elements of a female homoerotic devotional tradition. Crawshaw could represent Teresa as receiving erotic 'darts' not merely from Christ but also from the Virgin Mary. Catherine of Sienna urged her sisters to put on the nuptial garment of Jesus whose body is represented as female and maternal.[33] Leo Steinberg has drawn attention to the sexualisation of Jesus in Renaissance art arguing that the baby Jesus touching his genitals or displaying an erection draws attention to the mystery of the incarnation, the dead or dying Christ doing the same anticipates and promises the resurrection.[34] I shall argue later on in the book that it is in the very nature and praxis of Christianity to cause gender trouble, to subvert notions of masculinity and femininity, to suggest alternative possibilities to heterosexuality. By positioning gay people, including gay Christians, against the Church or in exile from the Church, gay liberationists too quickly and too easily cut themselves off from possible theological resources for dealing with the issue of identity.

Exodus as an imagery implies a calling out, a release into something better. For Cleaver gay people have been called out of secrecy and silence into freedom and with that freedom comes a new name 'gay' and the creation of a new type or class of person. He recognises that the category of homosexual is a social construct but believes that God is taking that social construct and redeeming it into a class, a class of lovers who stand in solidarity with others who are oppressed, Christian and non-Christian. But how this class relates to the wider ek-klesia, the heirs to the exodus and the new exodus of the resurrection is not clear. Cleaver never explicitly states that gay people are called out of the Church but there are implicit hints. He argues that it is important to find a liturgical 'room of our own'[35] and practice ministry rather than waiting for the Church to give permission.[36] But what Cleaver has not really grasped even though he makes the point again and again is that the Church is precisely an exodus community in which a ragbag of people carrying socially constructed identities such as Gentiles, Samaritans, eunuchs, prostitutes etc. are given a new identity which transcends and subverts such identities. The Church is *the* exodus community, one may be put out and to be put out of it is always to be expelled illegitimately and sinfully, but one cannot be called out of it, one can only be called further into it, to wrestle for a recognised place perhaps. Exile implies a putting out or a being driven out. Exile may be a place of discovery, a place of revelation but it is always a strange land, which the exiled occupies reluctantly longing for home. It may be that among some lesbian and gay Christians the exile does not hurt enough because it has actually ceased to be an exile and become instead an alternative ecclesial and social space, an exodus, and lesbian and gay people are then in danger of losing a sense of their own otherness, their own prophetic part in a theo-social world constructed around heterosexuality. Gay and lesbian Christians must not be too quick to leave the Church for the Church is the exodus still struggling, as the gay community is still struggling, to adjust to its radical freedom and the internal dynamics of being a new class of people.

There are also occasions when gay liberation theology comes perilously close to repeating the mistakes of gay liberal theology. Theology is reduced to hermeneutics and to ethics and boiled so powerfully in the pain of gay 'experience' that in some cases it appears to disappear altogether along with the divine who like the Cheshire cat fades away in face of its own benevolent immanence. The advocacy of a radically immanent divine presence also grates against the Latin American liberationist paradigm which acknowledges that our only hope is in a God who is control of history and who moves it in the direction of liberation. Radical immanentism requires a naively romantic view of gay identity and gay lives. It ultimately leaves us all to pull ourselves up by our bootstraps. But any involvement in political activism for any length of time will make the Christian activist sceptical of human ability to realise the values of the kingdom unaided. Also one of the lessons of the AIDS crisis is how easily the fruits of years of activism can be wiped out. If we are not ultimately dependent upon God in our struggles for liberation, if at the end of the rainbow there is not an ultimate NO to oppression it is hard to work out why we should be doing theology at all.

Notes

1   J. Michael Clark, *A Place to Start: Toward an Unapologetic Gay Liberation Theology* (Dallas: Monument Press, 1989).

2   Clark, *A Place to Start*, p. 15.

3   Clark, *A Place to Start*, p. 44.

4   Clark, *A Place to Start*, pp. 71–2.

5   Clark, *A Place to Start*, p. 77.

6   Clark, *A Place to Start*, pp. 148–9.

7   Clark, *A Place to Start*, pp. 170–171.

8   J. Michael Clark, *A Defiant Celebration: Theological Ethics and Gay Sexuality* (Garland: Tangelwüld Press, 1990).

9   Clark, *A Defiant Celebration*, p. 36.

10 Clark, *A Defiant Celebration*, p. 72.

11 J. Michael Clark, *Beyond Our Ghettos: Gay Theology in Ecological Perspective* (Cleveland: The Pilgrim Press, 1993).

12 Clark, *Beyond Our Ghettos*, p. 10.

13 Clark, *Beyond Our Ghettos*, p. 48.

14 J. Michael Clark, *Defying the Darkness: Gay Theology in the Shadows* (Cleveland: The Pilgrim Press, 1997).

15 Clark, *Defying the Darkness*, p. 42.

16 Clark, *Defying the Darkness*, pp. 80–86.

17 Gary David Comstock, *Gay Theology Without Apology* (Cleveland: The Pilgrim Press, 1993).

18 Comstock, *Gay Theology Without Apology*, p. 4.

19 Comstock, *Gay Theology Without Apology*, p. 9.

20 Comstock, *Gay Theology Without Apology*, p. 12.

21 Comstock, *Gay Theology Without Apology*, p. 57.

22 Comstock, *Gay Theology Without Apology*, p. 99.

23 Richard Cleaver, *Know My Name: A Gay Liberation Theology* (Louisville: Westminster John Knox Press, 1995).

24 Daniel T. Spencer, *Gay and Gaia: Ethics, Ecology, and the Erotic* (Cleveland: The Pilgrim Press, 1996), p. 368.

25 Sallie McFague, *Models of God: Theology for an Ecological, Nuclear Age* (Philadelphia: Fortress Press, 1987) and *The Body of God: An Ecological Theology* London: SCM, 1993).

26 Bernadette J. Brooten, *Love Between Women: Early Christian Responses to Female Homoeroticism* (Chicago and London: University of Chicago Press, 1996).

27 Spencer, *Gay and Gaia*, pp. 109–10.

28 Spencer, *Gay and Gaia*, p.123.

29 Spencer, *Gay and Gaia*, p. 126.

30 Rosemary Radford Ruether, *Gaia and God: An Ecofeminist Theology of Earth Healing* (New York: HarperCollins, 1992).

31 Richard Rambuss, *Closet Devotions* (Durham and London: Duke University Press, 1998).

32 See also Pat Pinsent, '"My Joy, My Love, My Heart": Sexuality and the Poems of George Herbert', in Michael A. Hayes, Wendy Porter and David Tombs (eds), *Religion and Sexuality* (Sheffield: Sheffield Academic Press, 1998), pp. 135–44.

33 Richard Rambuss, *Closet Devotions*, pp. 41, 47–8.

34 Leo Steinberg, *The Sexuality of Christ in Renaissance Art and in Modern Oblivion* (New York: Pantheon, 1983).

35 Cleaver, *Know My Name*, p. 117.

36 Cleaver, *Know My Name*, p. 107.

Chapter 4

Erotic Theology

Lesbian theology developed as a distinct body of theology in primary relationship with feminist rather than gay male liberal or liberationist theology. The influence of gay male theology upon lesbian theology is minimal but lesbian theology has had an enormous influence on gay liberationist theology as gay liberationist theologians sought to acknowledge and respect the 'difference' of lesbians. The most influential lesbian feminist theologian is undoubtedly Carter Heyward, Episcopalian priest and latterly Howard Chandler Robbins Professor of Theology at the Episcopal Divinity School, Cambridge, Massachusetts. The theology she has crafted in a substantial body of work has attained the status of orthodoxy in gay and lesbian theology in that some of her theories and concepts are repeated uncritically as truth. Chief among these is her identification of the divine with the erotic.

The Erotic and/as Divine

Touching Our Strength remains Heyward's most comprehensive reflection upon sexuality.[1] To comprehend Heyward's theology we must look behind it to the work of the black lesbian feminist poet Audre Lorde on the erotic. Lorde set out to try and reclaim the concept of the erotic from patriarchy which had reduced it to 'the confused, the trivial, the psychotic, the plasticised sensation'.[2] Lorde identified the erotic with a deep body knowledge and a drive towards joy, satisfaction and self-fulfilment which may be encountered in sexual relations but may also be experienced 'in dancing, building a bookcase, writing a poem, explaining an idea'.[3] The erotic is our 'yes' within ourselves, our deepest cravings but we have been taught to fear these and to repress them, to rely upon external authorities rather than our deep internal knowledge, our 'erotic guides'. Once, however, we learn to live out of the erotic and to recognise our deepest feelings and needs 'we begin to give up, of necessity, being satisfied with suffering, and self-negation, and with the numbness which so seems like their only alternative in our society'.[4]

Lorde's influence upon Heyward is acknowledged and obvious. Heyward, however, develops Lorde's concept of the erotic in two ways. First, Heyward emphasises that the erotic is 'our power in relation' and second, Heyward identifies that power with God.

> God is our relational power. God is born in his relational power. God is becoming our power insofar as we are giving birth to his sacred Spirit in the quality of our lives in relation, the authenticity of our mutuality, the strength of our relational matrix. It is a paradox: God is becoming our relational matrix insofar as we are the womb in which God is being born. This may be easier to comprehend if we substitute the word 'love' for 'God'.[5]

This God calls us to live in right relationship with others, to avoid absorption either into our own selves or into others, to build relationships of mutuality. Mutuality and equality are not the same. Equality implies an identical status between partners which is difficult to achieve under contemporary hierarchical structures. Mutuality however 'is a vision of justice in which by the power of God, we call one another forth into our most liberating, creative possibilities. Mutuality, unlike equality, signals relational growth and change and constitutes an invitation into shaping the future together'.[6] Unequal relationships like those between parents and children and people of different races may be mutual relationships if both partners are committed to growing and changing in relation to each other and fighting against those structures that lock people into relations of inequality. This is why for lesbians and gay men coming out is such an important theological statement, it is an acknowledgement of the central importance of the erotic in our lives and a statement of resistance to unjust power relations. It is a statement of disassociation from dominant political, social and theological discourses.

Heyward adopts a social constructionist approach towards sexual identity because of her focus on relationality. Relationality presupposes relativity because everything is relative to everything else, nothing is static – we become who we are in relationship to others. Thus Heyward reveals a certain debt to process theology. Also a historical reading of sexuality alerts us to the dynamics of power at the basis of various constructions of sexual identity and therefore we understand what must be done to create relationships based upon mutuality. What a historical reading of sexuality reveals most clearly is that heterosexism is the ideological foundation of western culture. It is heterosexism and the structures of 'power-over' that spew from it that are challenged by the erotic. But we live under, are shaped by and act out the structures of sadomasochism, domination and alienation and there is a constant tension between the power of the erotic and the power of alienation. Heterosexism underpins most Christian theology. It is enshrined in the concept of natural law but it also evident in most liberal theology which tends to place God above the fray of socio-economic life whilst at the same time individualising spirituality and universalising experience. The God of theism dislikes women and gay people, the God of liberalism is above such concerns. Ethics are reduced to individual opinion. Different opinions are tolerated but dominant structures and discourses are unchallenged. The God of right-relation is a God who takes sides and encourages all to do the same. S/he is a god intimately involved because s/he is the power of right relation, the eros that drives us towards each other in right relation. S/he is the source of transcendence because s/he calls us forth from and 'out' of ourselves towards others. In right relationship we not only experience God as the power of right relation we also 'god', we bring God forth.

A theology of right relation requires a different understanding of authority from that which has dominated in Christian theological discourse. Something has authority for us if it evokes something we already know, or have or are – namely mutuality. Nothing has authority over us by right. But neither is the liberal Enlightenment notion of internal authority acceptable for it does not give birth to mutuality either, just individualism. So scripture is only holy and authoritative in so far as those who read and use it do so as part of a commitment to mutuality and justice.

An understanding of the divine as erotic power requires a sex-affirming ethic in which non-abusive sexual pleasure is a moral good. Such an ethic has to be worked out against the grain of the Christian tradition because, 'the shaping of a humane, body-affirming, relational ethics of sexuality … is not an enterprise in which traditional Christianity has either experience or knowledge'.[7] The first step is to recognise our connectedness so that when one person suffers the whole is affected. Goodness and virtue are not individual qualities but gifts to be shared and held together in friendship. Such friendship requires faithfulness, 'this faith involves trusting that each of us is being honest with the other; that each knows and cares about the other on the basis of who she really is, rather than on the basis simply of who we might wish her to be; and that each desires the other's well-being'.[8] Such faithfulness is manifested in different types of commitment to different people, 'taking care' of the particular relationship through negotiation and honouring each other's feelings. Being faithful involves being real in our relationships, honest and open and present. Fidelity may ultimately involve a letting go. All this applies to all our relationships all of which are the creation of and open to the transformation of the erotic. In our sexual relationships the erotic seeks to redeem and transform its perversion into the pornographic, in which sexual desire is constructed as shameful and antithetical to the divine and becomes a place of individual satisfaction. It is only possible to overcome this pornographic culture by daring to love in the power of the divine. Living in such power opens up rather than closes down the possible configuration of relationships. Monogamy may be chosen as the best way to 'take care' of a primary relationship, a relationship in which the erotic is most obviously present. But monogamy may also be 'a smokescreen behind which partners, or spouses, shield their real feelings, fear, yearnings and relational questions … a commitment to monogamy can, and often does, prevent honest engagement, struggle, and growth in a relationships'.[9] The choice is not between monogamy and promiscuity but between monogamy and sexual friendships and in any and all these relationships we are obliged to be faithful and to manifest the seven chief qualities of right relation: *Courage* in which we dare to go beyond our fear into a place of vulnerability for the sake of the erotic, it is to take a chance on right relationship. *Compassion* which is the embodied knowledge that our lives are connected. It manifests itself in solidarity and humility. *Anger* which is again an embodied form of knowledge which 'signals the depth and strength of our desire to be friends'.[10] It is a signal feeling, a gut reaction against wrong relationship. *Forgiveness* is 'an empowering response to woundedness and disconnection. It is our release from the stranglehold of the past and from stuckness in feelings of shame or guilt, remorse or resentment'.[11] Real forgiveness requires humility on all parts. It involves the 'guilty' accepting their guilt and vowing to change and being accepted as brothers and sisters by the wounded. Forgiveness involves a recognition of our radical connection with one another. It also involves forgiving ourselves. Forgiveness is essential to the reality at the basis of fidelity. *Touching* when it takes place in right relationship is an experience of transcendence. In such a context it is sacramental. *Healing* which is an embodied commitment to all living creatures, to honesty, fidelity and eros. And finally *faith* which is an affirmative response to eros in the face of structures that seek to prevent right relationship.[12]

Heyward's theology is impressively non-individualistic. She manages to centre the divine in the midst of human relationship without identifying the divine with human relationships. Unlike gay liberation theologians she claims no particular epistemological privilege for lesbian and gay relationships nor does she write out of a sexual identity as such but she writes from a place into which her experience as a lesbian has led her. It has led her to a reconstruction of God as erotic power. She does not isolate sexual relationships from all other relationships but seeks to fashion a common ethic for all relationships. She also acknowledges the constraints that all of us work under in trying to realise mutuality within relationships. But some of the weaknesses of her approach are evident in her extraordinary book *When Boundaries Betray Us*.[13] This book is a painfully detailed account of Heyward's relationship with her therapist. The book is first of all a testimony to the psychological strain put on anyone who tries to live an authentic lesbian life in the Church. Heyward went into therapy because she was exhausted. Initially Heyward found her therapy with a lesbian therapist enormously healing. She felt the power of the erotic, the divine, moving between her and her therapist. However, Heyward's therapist refused to consider becoming friends with Heyward after the therapy ended on the grounds that to do so would be to violate professional boundaries. Heyward refused to accept this because her experience of erotic power was so real and she experienced her therapist's rejection of the possibility of friendship as abusive. The book is an attempt to argue that sometimes the boundaries created to protect the vulnerable can actually serve to stifle the power of erotic between persons. Heyward's experiences draw attention to the dangers that emerge from associating God with erotic power and mutuality in right relation or indeed of associating the divine with any sort of human feeling, emotion or desire. The danger is that we identify the divine with *our* feelings and use the language of mutuality, friendship and faithfulness to justify our own will-to-power in relationships.

Heyward is highly critical of liberal theology but she in fact exemplifies some of the classic features of liberal theology. For Heyward Christian doctrine is secondary to experience and praxis, indeed it must be expressive of those things. This is particularly evident in her most recent book which is a work of Christology. Reprising many of the themes of her previous works Heyward argues that the defining aspect of Jesus' ministry was his demonstration that God was not above or beyond humanity but with us and between us. In his life he demonstrated the *dunamis* of God, the uncontrollable power of right relationship, and it is this power that is available for all of us to share. Jesus' significance lies not in his difference from us but in similarity to us, which makes christic living a possibility for all of us.[14] As a lesbian feminist she cannot recognize a dualism between male and female, sexuality and spirituality, gay and straight, and in the same way she cannot recognize a dualism between divinity and humanity which can only be miraculously combined in one unique individual. Rather what the Jesus story teaches us is that all human beings are capable of manifesting divine power. She advocates what she calls a 'we, not he' Christology. Heyward marries this classically liberal Christology with a postmodern celebration of relativity to oppose what she labels 'moralism', the belief that we alone are right and have an obligation to make others see things the same way. The Religious Right have made Jesus into a moralistic deity and Jesus must be rescued from this because Jesus did not live a life of moralism but a life of passion. To live a life of passion is to 'come out' for justice-love to stand in solidarity with the poor, oppressed and marginalized, it is to break boundaries in order that people might have life, it is to live out of faith. People who live out of passion are people who make atonement, which is the making of right relationship with God but such people are always incarnating right relation in the midst of wrong relation and so will suffer for it. This is what happened to Jesus. The traditional doctrine of atonement is an expression of patriarchy – the sadistic father handing over his son to be tortured and die. It can have no place in a theology of right relation. Rather Jesus' story is the story of our common body.

The erotic in Heyward's theology is foundational but does she like Schleiermacher build a theology on the basis of an experience most of us have not had? Though she would blame a lack of such experience on the structures we live under. But who has the authority to determine what enhances mutuality and what does not? The friends themselves? But Heyward's practice seems to suggest that it is in fact the individual. In addition Kwok Pui-Lan has drawn attention to the difficulty non-western women have with the language and the concept of the erotic because for them the erotic is identified with abusive sexuality.[15]

Heyward's construction of the divine as erotic power has been widely embraced within gay and lesbian theology. It is incorporated uncritically into the work of Clark, Spencer, Goss, and others. It is for example, accepted and developed by Anne Bathurst Gilson in her attempt to construct a feminist theo-ethical liberation theology. Gilson argues that the Church's traditional prioritising of agape over eros is a crucial part of its disconnection of the sexual from the divine, a disconnection that led to the eroticisation of violence. She takes on board uncritically Heyward's concept of the erotic but does seek to answer some of the questions that she feels Heyward did not address. She feels that Heyward underestimated the reality of eroticised violence which is not only encountered in the fact that justice and equality are not considered 'sexy' in western culture but also in the construction of homosexuality and heterosexuality in such a way as to encourage or incite violence towards gay and lesbian people. Eroticised violence blocks our ability to experience mutuality. One way in which to resist such violence is to learn to know ourselves and love ourselves. Linking God and eros is important in overcoming self-hatred, enabling us to name ourselves and giving us confidence in our ability to 'bodyforth' the divine.[16] God participates in sex, we often involuntarily call forth God's presence at the height of our bodily ecstasy, and God is actively present in our love making calling us into mutuality and justice. More than this we participate in God's sexuality which is directed towards us, 'God is moved by our moving. God is changed by our changing. God is touched by our touching. As we love our neighbours as ourselves, we incarnate God and love Her. And She loves us back'.[17] When we are able to accept this, to acknowledge the presence of the sacred in our bodies and our love making then we are better able to acknowledge the sacred in the bodies of those around us and we also become increasingly affronted by and spurred to action against any eroticised violence. Thus we begin to engage in the process of reconnecting what has been disconnected, engaging in practices of solidarity and trying to understand the relations between different types of oppression. This involves a literal reconnection between groups of oppressed people that have been kept apart. Sexual connecting, moving through our fears of loving ourselves to relationships of mutuality is a resource for wider political strategies of reconnection. Thus we can move from surviving to thriving, from resisting the day-to-day experiences of oppression to active involvement in the building of a different world. Part of this involves turning the Church from an agape community into an eros community, a community yearning for erotic mutuality and embodied justice and in which the sexual is understood as a life-enhancing way in which to learn and express love of God, self and neighbour. This will be a Church in which lesbian and gay people are not discriminated against, inclusive language would be used in the liturgy and the sexual would be celebrated, erotic violence condemned and structures would be created to enable people to engage in active listening. The creation of such a Church requires a lot of daring behaviour on the part of those who share this vision of an eros community but Gilson believes the time has now come to dare to risk eros breaking free.

Virginia Ramey Mollenkott is a lesbian feminist theologian from an evangelical background whose work always bears the marks of her profession as a professor of English. She seeks to construct a 'sensuous spirituality' deeply rooted in scripture and centred around the notion of eros as a spiritual urge which she takes from Lorde and Heyward.[18] Mollenkott finds in the Song of Songs a celebration of the connection between the erotic and the divine in a non-marital relationship and in the various configurations of 'family' relationship that are presented in the Bible (Mollenkott lists forty) which vary from the patriarchal extended family to the same-sex partnership of Naomi and Ruth. Mollenkott has recently shifted to a queer theological perspective and we shall encounter her again when we examine that branch of theology. The point I am trying to make at this stage is that Heyward's construction of the divine has simply been adopted by theologians uncritically and worked up, expanded and rooted but not questioned.

Just Good Friends

Heyward regards friendship as

> a synonym for right, mutual, relation. This is because, for many women, friendship is the most exact experience we have of mutual relationship. For many of us, heterosexual as well as lesbian, our friendships with women, whether lovers or not, are more genuinely erotic that our marriages or relationships with male lovers.[19]

This is a view shared by the lesbian feminist theologian and co-founder of the Women's Alliance for Theology, Ethics and Ritual, Mary E. Hunt. Hunt claims that friendship has received little attention as a theme in the Christian tradition which has identified salvation with suffering and this has had the serious effect of undermining the moral agency of oppressed groups who do not have the choice as to whether to engage in acts of self sacrifice. Hunt argues that friendship provides a more empowering foundation upon which to build our lives. Women are the experts in this field and so have much to teach the Church and world. Drawing upon specific stories of women's friendships Hunt argues that friendship blows apart the key elements of heterosexism:

> A friendship norm implies new patterns of relating that reflect values of love and justice lived out not two by heterosexual two, but in many combinations of genders and in threes, fours, and dozens as well .... Models of church and community that are based on coupling (whether homosexual or heterosexual) and on limited notions of family need to be re-examined.[20]

Furthermore, women's experience of friendship with animals and the earth undermines the patriarchal dualism between nature and culture.

Hunt identities four elements of women's friendship which she fashions into a model of right relation. When these four elements are held in balance right relationship results, when friendships go wrong it is because they are out of balance. The first element is love which Hunt defines as 'an orientation toward the world as if my friend and I were more united than separated, more at one among the many than separate and alone'.[21] Power, the second element, is the ability for friends to make choices for themselves, for their children and with their community. This involves a commitment on the part of friends to struggle against structural systems that prevent some being able to have such power as well as loving each other into personal power. A lack of balance in power is the most common reason for friendship to end. The third element is embodiment. Everything we do involves our bodies and our bodies impact in various ways on each other. Hunt considers sexual expression a human right, not a heterosexual privilege, 'thus, sex between friends, if/when both are consenting, careful, and committed to the well-being of themselves and one another, has everything to recommend it'.[22] Women in the western world have been taught to despise their bodies and friends have a duty to teach each other of the beauty of their bodies. Friendships will be always be generative – the love between friends flowing out and expanding to encompass more and more people. Friendships may end because of different embodied choices – one may want to spend more time together than the other or want to be physically intimate in a manner that the other does not. The final element is spirituality which Hunt defines as 'making choices about the quality of life for oneself and for one's community'.[23] It involves attending to things like how we bury our dead and what films, theatre and music we encourage. Though particular friendships, our best friendships, are particularly intense forms of these elements we should be cultivating friendship towards everyone and everything. The loss of a friend can be as painful as a divorce or bereavement and just as inexplicable, made more painful by the fact that society does not acknowledge the value of friendship. Such loss teaches us that there is a sense in which we are radically alone and hence the importance of befriending ourselves. It also reminds us that because nothing is permanent no one can be 'owned' and also that friendship is to some extent a pure matter of luck or, to put it more theologically, grace. The great value of friendship as a model of right relation is that it is available to all (unlike marriage) but can also be cultivated within pre-existing relationships like marriage. Friendships are qualitative not quantative experiences, friendships may change and end – like childhood friendships or partnerships – but we must learn to value in memory the latter as we tend to do the former. Hunt acknowledges the limits of her model. First it does not do justice to the mysterious nature of friendship, the point at which it defies irrational explanation. Second, it is a model that has been constructed out of women's experience and it is unclear as to whether it can be applied to men or indeed to women of different classes, races and cultures. And finally Hunt admits that it is yet unclear whether the model is a practical one, whether it will facilitate friendship.

Hunt believes that it is vital to 'sacramentalise' friendship, by which she means pay it attention through public expression both by celebrating its formation and commemorating its loss. This will encourage communities to take friendship seriously and make us accountable for them. But it is important that this does not take the form of imitating heterosexual coupledom, it is important to celebrate friendships in their plurality and one-to-one commitments must acknowledge this fact. We are all called into 'unlikely coalitions' of 'justice-seeking friends' and one example of such a coalition is women-church, women coming together in base communities, sacramentalising their experience and working against injustice.

Finally, Hunt turns to some explicit theological reflection upon friendship. Imaging God as a divine friend is helpful. It is a personable but not intrusive image. Better still the divine should be imaged as friends, just as friends never exist in the singular neither can the divine friend and 'there may even be a hint of this insight in the Christian trinitarian theologies'.[24] Friendship also teaches something about the nature of divinity,

> Theologically a divinity that overarches all that is, remains static even as people change, is unnecessary. To the contrary, loss of friends teaches that being alone is inevitable, that even the divine abandons people, or so it seems … . Who wants a divinity that does not measure up to reality? Loss shows that being radically alone, even without a divine friend, is an experience one can survive. A God who is absent is a venerable yet vulnerable part of the Christian tradition.[25]

Three distinctive characteristics of women's friendships, generativity, attention and community and their convergence in justice also reveal something about the divine nature. God as friend is the one who stands on the side of the oppressed 'with open arms and amble bosom ready to embrace and to nurture as necessary, to propel and encourage as appropriate'.[26]

Hunt produces an impressive analysis of women's friendships that in itself serves to sacramentalise friendship which is an undervalued relationship in contemporary western culture. She constructs a friendship-ethic that incorporates and applies to all forms of sexual and non-sexual relationship that unites all regardless of sexuality and gender in a common project of building a just world. However, for something that styles itself as a 'feminist theology of friendship' there is remarkably little theological reflection her work. Like Heyward and many other gay and lesbian theologians Hunt seems to dismiss the Christian tradition as irredeemably patriarchal and heterosexist and yet it is just not true that friendship has not been valued in the Christian tradition. As Michael Vasey has noted the valorisation of male friendship was a key feature of pre-modern Christianity and the undervaluing of friendship one of the most distinctive marks of modern Christianity.[27] Also much like Clark Hunt's divine friend(s) is a process God who easily disappears being so identified with human action and agency that s/he fades into the background of the discussion which is ethical rather than theological in character.

Elizabeth Stuart, on the other hand, offers a theology of friendship much more overtly theological and routed in the Christian tradition than Hunt or Heyward.[28] Stuart believes that it is time that lesbian and gay Christians reclaimed the ball of their lives that has been kicked around for too long by Church assemblies and synods and follow the example of Latin American liberation Christians in claiming the right to reflect theologically upon their own experience. The scriptures testify to the fact that the incarnation continues through the Spirit/Paraclete in people, in the community of Jesus' followers, not in texts. When Christians disagree all one can do is be patient and wait to see who is right. Stuart believes that in terms of the Church's debate on homosexuality we are in a waiting time. All that lesbian and gay Christians can do is take our own experience, share it, analyse it and spin it into threads of knowledge which can be woven with the threads of others. We cannot know whether a pattern will emerge. If it does, we may claim it as a moment of revelation, a pattern, a map a trace of the divine.[29]

Like Heyward Stuart identifies the God who speaks through experience with Sophia/ Hochma of the wisdom tradition, the immanent presence of the divine in creation, pervading and penetrating all things. But this God cannot be trapped in the tapestries of experience that we weave, she has already moved on summoning us into greater truth and therefore we must be careful not to identity our experience and interpretation of it with the truth.

Stuart builds her theology upon sociological evidence that lesbian and gay people tend to define their relationships in terms of friendship. She analyses the construction of friendship across the ages (including in her analysis a number of theologians such as Aelred of Rievaulx) noting that certain themes emerge. First friendship can only exist between equals but can also sometimes 'break rank' uniting people in friendship who are structured into inequality. Second, friendship is the means by which we discover and learn to love ourselves. And third, a distinctive aspect of female and gay reflection on friendship is the acknowledgement of an erotic dimension to it. This subverts the clear lines often drawn between *agape* and *eros* in modern Christian literature. Stuart utilises the concept of the erotic drawn from Lorde and Heyward but not uncritically. She dislikes the implication in Lorde's writing that the erotic is an inherent knowledge within women waiting to be uncovered because this suggests a gender essentialism which Stuart being a social constructionist cannot accept. She argues that what Lorde identifies as the erotic is a power created between people, a love that is born of love. However, she also argues that the language of the erotic is unfortunate because in western and western-influenced culture the erotic is the language of sex and sex is experienced as an expression of dominance and submission by many women. Stuart prefers to identify the power of the erotic with 'passion' (as Heyward does in her latter work) because it,

is one of those rare words which we use in love-talk which has not been reduced to genital activity. It encompasses within its widely accepted meanings a strong force driving a person outwards, anger, enthusiasm, pain and violence ... as well as sexual love in the narrowest sense of that term – all elements of the 'erotic' as Lorde conceived it.[30]

It is also appropriate because it is a term that has historically been linked with friendship in the passionate friendships between women which are a characteristic of eighteenth-century upper class British culture.

Stuart's point is the same as that of Hunt and Heyward, passion is at the basis of all our loving relationships and is most appropriately articulated in friendship which must be the ethical basis of all our relationships. She is deeply resistant to the construction of lesbian and gay relationships as marriages. The Churches have turned marriage into an idol by claiming that it is the ideal Christian relationship. The result is a failure to deal with the fact that marriage has been constructed as an unequal and privatised relationship from biblical times onwards and in contemporary western society is failing spectacularly. Stuart argues that an alternative reading of scripture reveals a people formed and sustained through sexual subversion. The stories of Ruth and Naomi, Tamar and David and Bathsheba flout levitical laws but in each case further God's purposes. The Song of Songs subverts the story of Eden, the story of David and Jonathan which 'bristles with ambiguity' presents us with a passionate covenant relationship for which there is no established means of description. The gospels present Jesus as a passionate, subversive man who declared that marriage and blood kinship had no ultimate status and that Isaiah's prediction of the inclusion of the eunuch (who was not an a-sexual person but a third sex renown for having passive sex with men) was coming true and himself left only one model of relating, that of friendship.

When she comes to teasing out some of the ethical implications of her model of relationships Stuart argues that one other advantage of using the language of passion is that it contains within it the notion of tragedy and pain. It is part of the tragedy of the human condition that we are socially constructed and formed by our environment in a context which has as 'its relational heart domination and submission'.[31] This means that we must avoid the temptation to be over optimistic as to what can be achieved in terms of relationships. Negotiating and balancing all friendship is hard but sexual relationships present particular problems:

> I believe that in the secret places of our lives we yearn for relationships based upon mutuality, justice, compassion and complete affirming acceptance. But for that yearning to be fulfilled, complete and utter vulnerability, radical vulnerability, must exist between the friends.[32]

Such radical vulnerability is a process which requires enormous effort, time and a safe environment in a cultural context which will seek to interrupt and scupper the process. Stuart believes that it is hard, if not impossible, to sustain more than one relationship of radical vulnerability at a time. Unlike many lesbian and gay theologians Stuart does not want to see celibacy devalued as a form of friendship in contemporary Christianity. In the context of a theology of friendship a celibate is

> someone who sacrifices the relationship of passionate radical vulnerability in order to commit themselves completely to the building up of a community of friendship. This means that their experience and practice of intimacy will be different. Whilst most of us intensify our friendship into a handful of close relationships, the celibate's intensity will be spread much further. Just as most of us constrict the expression of our passion because of our finiteness, so celibates constrict their experience of radically vulnerable relationships in order to be able to be faithful to a community.[33]

In the final chapter Stuart turns her attention to the understanding of God as friend. Unlike Hunt, however, Stuart wants to start with the Christian tradition itself and more particularly with the doctrine of the Trinity. Taking her cue from liberation theologians she constructs the Trinity as a community of friends whose mutuality and difference is preserved using the concept of *perichōrēsis* from John of Damascus which conjures up a 'dynamic, non-hierarchical, equal, mutual relationship'.[34] The doctrine of the Trinity undermines heterosexual coupledom by presenting us with a same-sex three-person relationship in God.

Like Mollenkott, but unlike other lesbian feminist theologians, Stuart attempt to root a theology based upon lesbian experience in the Christian tradition. Though she is critical of an essentialist understanding of the erotic and advocates an social constructionist understanding of sexuality Stuart nevertheless shares with many lesbian and gay theologians the assumption that a lesbian or gay identity is stable enough to build a theology upon. Whilst espousing a social constructionist approach lesbian theologians also follow most feminist theologians in assuming that 'woman' is a concept stable enough to do theology with, that there is such a thing as women's experience, women's friendships and so on and whilst most are prepared to acknowledge differences wrought by class and race and sexual orientation, none are prepared to question the very categories of 'woman' and 'lesbian'. This is what queer theory questions and both Stuart and Mollenkott have more recently taken on board some of the challenges of queer theory.

Erotic Theology: An Assessment

One of the most incisive critiques of erotic theology has been made by the British theologian Linda Woodhead.[35] She argues that modernity has brought the privatisation and individualisation of sex which values pleasure above all else. She recognises that erotic theology is an attempt to break through the barriers of this privatisation and move sex into a wider relational and political context. However, Woodhead is extremely sceptical as to erotic theology's ability to achieve this. She believes at the base of erotic theology is still the pleasure of the individual:

> eros theology buys into the assumptions of modern individualism by making orgasmic experience foundational, the only thing 'thick' enough to ground relationships, society and religion. These latter do not have enough independent value and reality to stand on their own, but must be vivified and ontologised by eros. Indeed, in much eros theology even God becomes reducible to erotic experience.[36]

In which case there is always a danger that erotic theology will simply end up 'baptising' modern constructions of sexuality rather than challenging them. For Woodhead the value of the Christian tradition in matters of sexuality is that it has always understood sexuality to be a cultural product and,

> that it is the nurturing and perfection of these institutions which makes possible good behaviour and experience. On a Christian understanding, the entrance into true relationship with God and neighbour is made possible only by entrance into the church, the new community called into being by God. It is the body of Christ which forms the basis of a new society – not the body of the individual.[37]

But in erotic theology God is condensed to the power of right relation, the Church is simply of no account and the incarnation is reduced in a great deal of this theology to an understanding of the sacredness of all bodies and divorced from the life, death and resurrection of Christ. This reductionism reveals lesbian feminist theology to be still living in the shadow of theological liberalism even as it claims to distance itself from it.

Lesbian feminist theology shares with gay liberationist theology a methodological prioritising of experience. Post-liberal theology has drawn attention to the communal, cultural and post-linguistic nature of all experience which renders its usefulness as a foundation for theology problematic.[38] Theologies based upon experience have also been increasingly perceived as problematic by those who stand within them as they have become aware of the fact that any attempt to firm up concepts of experience to make them sufficiently strong to bear the weight of theology necessarily involves exclusion and therefore doing violence to the experience of others.[39] There is a danger that theologies based in experience end up either advocating a thinly disguised form of essentialism[40] or even, as with a liberationist approach when the experience focussed on is that of oppression, an identity based upon oppression and victimhood which, however hard it tries not to, tends to avoid issues of sin except as they apply to someone else.

Theologies based upon experience are also difficult for those who do not share that experience to grasp or to translate in a meaningful and not reductionist way into their own theological language. Thus experiential theologies can often become detached from the wider Christian community and ecclesial debates and theology itself becomes a Babel with different groups of Christians speaking out of their own experience but unable to communicate effectively with each other. Whilst they have been extremely effective in the deconstruction of dominant theologies they have generally been less successful in the reconstruction of theology, following liberal theology in a demythologising strategy that devalues tradition and can fail to appreciate its richness and diversity. They often follow modern liberalism in reducing theology to a system of ethics which, cut off from any kind of cosmology, can only compete alongside other ethical systems on equal terms. In other words theologies based upon experience often end up virtually ceasing to be theologies at all.

Notes

1   Carter Heyward, *Touching Our Strength: The Erotic as Power and the Love of God* (San Francisco: Harper and Row, 1989).
2   Audre Lorde, 'Uses of the Erotic: The Erotic as Power', in James B. Nelson and Sandra P. Longfellow (eds), *Sexuality and the Sacred: Sources for Theological Reflection* (London: Mowbray, 1994), pp. 75–9.
3   Lorde, 'Uses of the Erotic', p. 77.
4   Lorde, 'Uses of the Erotic, p. 78.
5   Heyward, *Touching Our Strength*, p. 24.
6   Heyward, *Touching Our Strength*, p. 34.
7   Heyward, *Touching Our Strength*, p. 125.
8   Heyward, *Touching Our Strength*, p. 129.
9   Heyward, *Touching Our Strength*, p. 136.
10 Heyward, *Touching Our Strength,* p. 143.
11 Heyward, *Touching Our Strength*, p. 145.
12 Heyward, *Touching Our Strength*, pp. 139–55.
13 Carter Heyward, *When Boundaries Betray Us: Beyond Illusions of What is Ethical in Therapy and Life* (San Francisco: HarperSanFrancisco, 1993).
14 Carter Heyward, *Saving Jesus From Those Who Are Right: Rethinking What it Means to be a Christian* (Minneapolis: Fortress Press, 1999). See also *Speaking of Christ: A Lesbian Feminist Voice* (New York: The Pilgrim Press, 1984).
15 Kwok Pui-Lan, 'The Future of Feminist Theology: An Asian Perspective', *The Auburn News* (Fall, 1992), n.p.

16 Anne Bathurst Gilson, *Eros Breaking Free: Interpreting Sexual Theo-Ethics* (Cleveland: The Pilgrim Press, 1995).
17 Gilson, *Eros Breaking Free*, p. 118.
18 Virginia Ramey Mollenkott, *Sensuous Spirituality: Out from Fundamentalism* (New York: Crossroad, 1993).
19 Heyward, *Touching Our Strength*, p. 188.
20 Mary E. Hunt, *Fierce Tenderness: A Feminist Theology of Friendship* (New York: Crossroad, 1991), p. 14.
21 Hunt, *Fierce Tenderness*, p. 100.
22 Hunt, *Fierce Tenderness*, p. 104.
23 Hunt, *Fierce Tenderness*, p. 105.
24 Hunt, *Fierce Tenderness*, p. 167.
25 Hunt, *Fierce Tenderness*, p. 132.
26 Hunt, *Fierce Tenderness*, p. 166.
27 Vasey, *Strangers and Friends*, pp. 80–112.
28 Elizabeth Stuart, *Just Good Friends: Towards a Theology of Lesbian and Gay Relationships* (London: Mowbray, 1995).
29 Stuart, *Just Good Friends*, p. 12.
30 Stuart, *Just Good Friends*, p. 89.
31 Stuart, *Just Good Friends*, p. 194
32 Stuart, *Just Good Friends*, p. 220.
33 Stuart, *Just Good Friends*, pp. 209–10.
34 Stuart, *Just Good Friends*, p. 242.
35 Linda Woodhead, 'Sex in a Wider Context', in Jon Davies and Gerard Loughlin (eds), *Sex These Days: Essays on Theology, Sexuality and Society* (Sheffield: Sheffield Academic Press, 1997), pp. 98–120.
36 Woodhead, 'Sex in a Wider Context', p. 105.
37 Woodhead, 'Sex in a Wider Context', p. 106.
38 George Lindbeck, *The Nature of Doctrine, Religion and Theology in a Postliberal Age* (Philadelphia: Westminster Press, 1984).
39 See Susan Brooks Thistlethwaite, *Sex, Race and God* (London: Geoffrey Chapman, 1990) and Mary McClintock Fulkerson, *Changing the Subject: Women's Discourses and Feminist Theology* (Minneapolis: Fortress Press, 1994).
40 In constructing a theology of friendship both Hunt and Stuart make huge claims about the nature of women's and gay experience which are impossible to substantiate. In arguing that lesbian and gay people tend to define their primary relationships in terms of friendship Stuart has to ignore or downplay the experiences of those who do not.

Chapter 5

AIDS and the Failure of Gay and Lesbian Theology[1]

Nothing has brought home to me the weaknesses of gay and lesbian theology (including my own work) than the manner in which it handled the AIDS crisis. My contention is that the claim of liberal, liberationist, feminist and gay and lesbian theologies to be based upon experience – either the universal experience of lesbian and gay people or the experience of oppression – is largely exposed as inaccurate when their reaction to AIDS is examined. This was not a failure that I noticed at the height of the AIDS pandemic in Europe and North America but something that has emerged from contemplation of a theory developed by Michael Vasey. Vasey claimed that gay men affected by HIV and AIDS had subverted the understanding and performance of death that dominates in contemporary western culture. He argued that

> The modern way of handling death is to call it 'natural' and ignore it as far as possible. Modern church life, despite the richness of its past theological and artistic tradition, has gone a long way towards accepting this view. Contemporary evangelical Christianity treats death as one of the accidents of life – to be responded to compassionately and passed over as quickly as possible.[2]

As well as utilising, 'gay skills in art, in celebration and in the voicing of anger, love and pain'[3] in the creation of funerals which articulate a non-natural, tragic understanding of death, Vasey believed that gay male responses to AIDS included a reconnection between desire and immortality, a connection which had characterised pre-Enlightenment understandings of death:

> The classic Christian imagination saw the awakening of love, the sweetness of sexual pleasure, and the fruitfulness of the sexual act as real but partial anticipations of the true locus of human longings for joy and immortality. The true and lasting fulfilment of these hopes lay in heaven. In a curious way the modern denial of heaven has simultaneously strengthened and weakened the relationship between sex and human preoccupation with desire and immortality.[4]

This hope in heaven as the fulfilment, the *telos* of human desire was lost when modernity shrunk desire and identified it with exclusively with heterosexual love thereby destroying the connection between desire, God and heaven precisely because the Church had bought into modernity's construction of sexual desire:

> Its [evangelical Christianity's] recurrent anxiety over 'family issues' is a measure of how deeply it has sold its soul to the destructive idols of Western culture: the reduction of the sense of beauty to 'heterosexual love' and the elimination of bonds of affection in the search for prosperity through the market.[5]

Vasey's conviction that AIDS had and would lead gay men to articulate a belief in the afterlife fascinated me because I had the impression that the subject of death and the afterlife was not one that particularly concerned gay and lesbian theologians. So I set up a research project to test Vasey's theory. My colleague, David Sollis, interviewed nine men who identified as gay, Christian and HIV positive and twenty-two men and women who had been involved as supporters to those living and dying with HIV/ AIDS in the UK. These included partners, friends, priests and pastors, and those who worked for support agencies. Through these supporters we gained access to the experiences of the literally thousands of men who were living with or who had died with HIV/AIDS. These interviews overwhelmingly confirmed Vasey's general theory. Gay men living with HIV/AIDS reflected upon their own mortality, planned their own funerals and had clear, well thought out and articulated beliefs in life after death. All of the men with HIV believed in a life after death. A number felt it was going to be so radically different that it was beyond description except through the use of biblical metaphors, particularly those found in Revelation. Others understood it as union with God. Two had been through some sort of mystical experience which convinced them of the existence of an afterlife. Andrew described his vision of 'the kingdom of heaven', which he experienced whilst seriously ill, in these terms, 'I experienced bliss, absolute joy and thought "yes this is it, I want to go there". There was a sort of skyline of a city but very indistinct ... I can only describe it as sort of expressionist ... and this beautiful warm golden light'.[6] Sollis found that the overwhelming majority of the HIV+ men were comfortable with the idea that death involved some sort of judgement. None of the interviewees were conscious of having received their beliefs through Church teaching. Although one, David, on reflection realised that he had:

> One of the most important things in terms of Christian faith and death, was the fact that Christ's ministry, his life, culminates at one point in his death and his resurrection ... it's funny isn't it when you say 'what does the Church teach?' – and you can forget the Church teaches that there is death and there is resurrection and that is fundamental stuff, and that does matter to me. Death makes sense if there is resurrection.[7]

The group of supporters also generally took the view that the majority of those gay men who died with AIDS had some sort of belief in the afterlife. The Revd. Elder Jean White of the Metropolitan Community Church believes that over ninety percent of the men she had ministered to who were atheists or agnostics when they were diagnosed came to some sort of belief in God and the afterlife,

> a spirituality sets in that perhaps they did not know they had. When you approach death you start looking at death in different ways and maybe you are more open to listening to your own inner self, and questioning things that you have never questioned before ... Sometimes I think we have a God sized blank and the nearer we go back to our creator we recognise it.[8]

Her claim was echoed by fellow MCC minister Neil Thomas who believes that AIDS engendered a deep spirituality in the lesbian and gay community as it focussed on issues of mortality and an Anglican priest, Malcolm Johnson, was struck by just how comfortable gay men were with discussing death, funerals and the afterlife. Another Anglican priest, Andrew Henderson, felt that he was never expected to confirm belief in the afterlife precisely because that belief was already so strong in the men he ministered to. Other ministers noted a strong belief in bodily resurrection. A number of supporters noticed the popularity of certain secular 'texts' such as Bette Midler's song 'The Rose' which articulate a sense of love stretching into eternity.

Lesbian and gay people became experts in death. One interviewee, Roy Parr, recalled a story about the space shuttle disaster of 1986,

> I am reminded of that story when the space shuttle blew up killing the crew there was an office which had televisions in every room broadcasting the news. When they saw the film on television they all crowded into the office of one of their managers who they knew was gay because they thought he could cope with it because he had friends who had died with HIV/AIDS ... They did a survey afterwards on why people went to him and it was because they thought he was the person to cope with it.[9]

Though the sample of interviewees was small and confined to the UK the evidence was consistent and impressive, AIDS led many gay men to reflect upon and believe in life after death. Sollis' research is supported by that of sociologists T. Anne Richards and Susan Folkman who interviewed 121 partners of gay men who had died of AIDS in San Francisco, one third of whom were HIV+ themselves. Fifty-four per cent of the interviewees made explicit reference to spiritual phenomena in their interviews and of those 74 per cent articulated this in terms of the spirit leaving the body and either joining friends or merging into the divine. Forty-three per cent of the participants who made reference to spiritual phenomena expressed the view that their relationship with their partner continued and some had direct communication with the deceased. Interestingly, HIV+ participants were more likely to report spiritual phenomenon that HIV-negative ones. Richards and Folkman's research also confirmed that gay men living with HIV/AIDS took control of their own funerals and memorials.[10]

Death hung like a pall over the lesbian and gay communities in the 1980s and 1990s until the advent of Combination Therapy in the late 1990s dramatically reduced the death rate. In the United States alone up until the end of 1999 425,357 people had lost their lives to AIDS, the vast majority being gay men.[11] In the year 1993 27,007 gay men died with AIDS in the USA, in 1994 the numbers rose to 28,673. In the UK, though the numbers are much smaller, numbers of deaths reached their peak in 1994 with around a thousand gay men dying that year. Between 1989 and 1997 nearly 7,000 gay men died with AIDS in the UK.[12] At the start of the pandemic men died quickly, too quickly to plan funerals, but as time went on and drugs like AZT bought some more time people did begin to think about their deaths and plan their own funerals. Lesbians were caught up in this nightmare as much as gay men. In the cultural construction of gay = AIDS = death, lesbians were implicated just as much as gay men and bore the social consequences. But AIDS also brought together lesbians and gay men in a common fight against ignorance and injustice and many lesbians gladly took on caring roles during this period.[13] Lesbians and gay men sat in hospitals together, went to funerals together and stared death in the face together. Is this experience reflected in gay and lesbian theology? What do these theologies have to say about death and the afterlife?

Gay Liberal Theology

Fortunato wrote a book specifically on the spiritual challenges of AIDS. On the one hand he argues that AIDS, by bolstering the already existing perception that because of their failure to reproduce gay people are associated with death, enables the declaration of the 'good news of mortality', a passionate love of life fuelled by an awareness of death. In other words, death teaches people the need to live life to the full now and gay people are learning that lesson through AIDS. But, on the other hand, Fortunato acknowledges that 'it would be unconscionable for a Christian to write a book about a fatal illness without discussing heaven'.[14] However he notes that heaven-talk is difficult in the contemporary western world in which religious belief is often collapsed into ethics, aesthetics and psychology and is countered by a literalist fundamentalism. However in searching for a means to talk about heaven Fortunato veers from a liberal theological approach to a more postmodern one and back again arguing that the breakdown of the metanarratives of the Enlightenment enables other forms of knowledge including intuitive knowledge to be taken seriously. But he also notes that the concept of curved time and space and the possibility of multiple worlds which quantum physics has postulated allows for the existence of a heavenly space. Refusing to speculate on the nature of heaven because all biblical texts ultimately affirm that we are dealing with a mystery impossible to comprehend, Fortunato is content to argue that our current existence cries out for fulfilment, for a return to the source of its life, God.

McNeill also addresses issues of mortality and the beyond in his work. Rather like Vasey, McNeill believes that AIDS could lead to a resumption of belief in bodily resurrection. Because gay men are so conscious of their embodiment, because they usually have no hope of living on in children, the only hope they may find acceptable is a resurrection hope.[15] Indeed, McNeill believes that 'scripture itself links the non-procreative status of lesbians and gays to the hope of resurrection'[16] in its promises to eunuchs in Isaiah 56.4–6 and Matthew 19.12. The doctrine of the resurrection needs to be proclaimed in the face of the horrors of AIDS because it is an affirmation that absolutely nothing can sever the bonds between God and us.

McNeill has no time for the feminist argument that the desire for immortality is a construction of the male ego. For McNeill the yearning for immortality is present in all human relationships, 'when two people give and receive genuine love, the happiness they find in this communion is expressed in a spontaneous longing for immortality. Every love poem ever written carries the message, "I am eternally yours!"'.[17] In fact it is the promise of immortality that makes 'the commitment of true, personal love' a possibility. Further, it is because gay men have already been through a journey of grief in the process of coming out, having to let go of the promises and rewards of hetero-society, that many with AIDS have died at peace assured of their own self-worth.[18]

Both Fortunato and McNeill deal with issues of immortality in a manner that is surprising for theologians I have consigned to the liberal camp. They do not attempt to demythologise or to merely rationalise. Perhaps this is because as psychotherapists and liberal theologians they are committed to taking people's experience seriously.

Glaser too has expressed a conviction that 'one of our callings as lesbian and gay Christians is to restore the Easter hope to a church that frequently echoes the scepticism of Thomas'.[19] But his theological reflections are more in line with what one would expect of a liberal theologian. He suggests that the concept of immortality Jesus directs us to in the parable of the good Samaritan is

> not an immortality based in personal preservation, personal safety, or an extended quality of life. Rather it is an immortality based in risking one's life to find it, chancing even death, whether on a robber-infested road or on a God-forsaken cross, to enrich the quality of life for others.[20]

So people who have died with AIDS 'live on in our hearts, having given us insights into AIDS, into life, into death itself, enabling us to care for ourselves and one another'.[21] Glaser characterises the process of judgement as a burning off of the chaff of our lives leaving only what is of value and this is what is saved, what is of value to others. God remembers what we did for love and forgets everything else. So for Glaser resurrection faith consists of simply being selectively remembered by God and by others.

Glaser's demythologisation and dis-enchantment of Christian doctrine is a classic liberal approach. Nevertheless these three liberal theologians have all been prompted by AIDS to face theological issues of death and the afterlife and McNeill and Fortunato do so in a manner that does not resort to demythologisation and this rather contradicts their obviously liberal approach in all other respects.

Gay Liberationist Theology

In all his work Clark is deeply concerned about the impact of AIDS upon the gay community and the challenges it poses. But like most gay and lesbian theologians he is more concerned with the ethical issues raised by AIDS than the theological ones. In *A Place to Start* Clark recognises that:

> Gay liberation theology ... must also wrestle with physical, natural suffering and dying (tragedy) and reach some understanding about death and about God's limitations in tragedy and death (theodicy). It will have to account for and bless our grief and our own constant confrontation with mortality and death.[22]

And that AIDS has made gay men 'reconsider our notions of life beyond death, aching because eternal life or reincarnation cannot undo the premature shortening of *this* life for our dying loved ones'.[23] Utilising process theology he comes to the conclusion that God exists as a fellow-sufferer in creation and that the chaotic nature of the universe means that things like AIDS will happen. This does not cast any doubt on the value of gay love nor on the value of people who have died, 'we must remember and hold on to the good of all these lives; this is also a part of what God is and does'.[24] God is not in any sense a Mr or Ms Fix-It but a companion in suffering. Thus, 'the resurrection as the focus of faith can in fact be displaced by the crucifixion as a symbolic locus of God's co-suffering activity'.[25] The resurrection is only of use as a symbol and metaphor of a community's resilience and resistance in the face of death and is only of use it is not taken literally.[26] Clark believes that literal concepts of immortality lead to a devaluing of this life. Here he is influenced by the work of feminist theologian Rosemary Radford Ruether who has argued that the growth of an other-worldly eschatological dimension in Christian history was an integral part of the development of what Clark calls 'a sexless, disembodied, male spirituality … devaluing the moral body in favour of the eternal immortal spirit'[27] and thereby devaluing women and all the sexually marginalised. For Clark any promises about life beyond death invalidate the value of gay lives before death. Thus Clark combines process and feminist insights to suggest that life beyond death for the individual does not exist but we are eternally remembered by the God, the matrix, whose collective personhood we are absorbed into.

These ideas are simply repeated in *A Defiant Celebration* and fleshed out a little more in *Beyond Our Ghettos* where Clark again follows various feminist theologians in arguing that any concept of life beyond death 'actually sanctions exhausting a clearly expendable earth'.[28] But by the time that Clark wrote *Defying the Darkness* circumstances had prompted him to rethink. Both he and his partner were now HIV+ and having to deal with the death of many friends. In addition another gay theologian, Ron Long, had challenged Clark's use of process theology arguing that even suggesting that God tolerates AIDS implicates God in the pandemic. Long is a radical postmodern gay theologian who argues that God is but the 'complex of anger' and 'spirit of resistance' and the hope for life after AIDS. Interestingly, because Long identifies God with hope he suggests that 'what cannot be imagined may nevertheless be the object of hope, a world so utterly transformed that lions lie down with lambs and the dead overflow in bodily delight'.[29] Clark was prompted to turn to the feminist theologian Kathleen Sands in order to articulate a theology more empathetic to the tragic dimensions of life.[30] It is then that Clark engages in a series of collapses and condensations. The line he previously drew between human and natural evil is erased and theology is collapsed into ethics, a transcendent, rescuing God is dismissed in favour of an immanent presence and life and death, goodness and evil are declared to be one. The only response to evil, suffering and tragedy is to dare to live anyway. In the closing pages of the book Clark declares,

> even though it feels very uncomfortable in the face of HIV/AIDS or any other chronic, life-threatening condition, I have become increasingly adamant about the very real possibility that this life may indeed be all there is … any reliance on validation or vindication in a 'next' world encourages us to devalue this world and this life – including all the companion life with which we share at the present moment – as only penultimate. A truly inclusive liberation theology, therefore, will not be focussed on the next world, but will articulate better ways to live in this one.[31]

Clark's position is endorsed by Spencer who also repeats the eco-feminist objections to belief in life after death. In the conclusion of his book Spencer takes up Clark's point that the AIDS pandemic made lesbian and gay people disposable, society as a whole was quite happy to let them die. This should give lesbian and gay people an empathetic relationship with the earth that has also been treated as dispensable and disposable.[32] But both Spencer and Clark seem to be prepared to tolerate the disposal and dispensability of the dead collapsed like the dinosaurs and the dodo to memory (albeit the divine memory) alone.

Comstock published his book in 1993 the year 27,007 gay men died with AIDS in the USA and yet his book seems curiously detached from the AIDS crisis. It opens with a description of Comstock's experience of buddying for a man dying with AIDS.

This man's defiant refusal to play the victim became a model for the unapologetic gay theology Comstock sought to develop but that is the most sustained analysis of AIDS the book contains.[33] His flattening out of the concept of salvation which is reduced to protest, resistance and right relationship and of resurrection to symbolise the indestructible nature of love, leaves him with no inclination or theological space for an afterlife.

Cleaver has more to say about AIDS than Comstock but has not got much to say about AIDS and death. In his discussion on the connection between gay male consciousness of embodiment and their active role in Christian liturgy he cites their creativity in constructing new rituals around death in the face of AIDS and he himself suggests adapting practices associated with the Mexican Day of the Dead for remembering those who have died with AIDS.[34] Cleaver has a great deal to say about the resurrection and makes much of it as a statement of the absolute value of the body and communal solidarity.[35] He declares that 'in the resurrection we are made free of death' but only explains that in terms of this life 'we are free too of the little deaths that oppressors try to inflict on us' because for Cleaver liberation must be an event in history.[36] Yet the eucharistic prayer Cleaver has written with which he ends his book 'to gather with all the holy lovers of our history and of our lives, around God's altar or around the coffee table of an AIDS hospice'[37] includes the lines,

> we call to mind those who have fallen asleep in your love, by hatred, by violence, accident, disease, or the merciful passing of time, and who are now waiting to greet us on the shore of the river we too one day must cross, especially those whose names we now offer ... and pray that all your people may at last in love be gathered from the four winds and the corners of the world, to rise as one body of Christ at the end of time.[38]

This suggests some belief in life after death and a final resurrection but it is a suggestion not elaborated upon in the theology that comes before.

Tim Morrison, who is an HIV trainer for a London health authority, demythologises life after death. The experience of the resurrection is the experience of joy in the face of suffering, sadness and death. It is also to play the Fool, to live unconstrained by the fear of death and social isolation and in the midst of the AIDS pandemic this is an experience that people need now not in the future.[39]

Gay liberationist theology when it deals with AIDS (and not all of it does) tends to reduce its challenge to ethics. AIDS does not challenge those theologians who buy into, repeat and reinforce eco-feminist 'orthodoxy' that belief in personal survival after death is a patriarchal obsession and bad for the earth, for women and for gay men. Those not influenced by eco-feminist theology seems to be paralysed by a liberationist commitment to life before death, as if taking into account the fact that as they wrote thousands upon thousands of gay men were facing issues of life after death would somehow undermine a liberationist agenda. Although it is worth noting that Latin American liberation theologians have tended not to abandon belief in life after death, a hope in the life to come being considered essential for, among other things, preventing an easy identification between earthly liberation and the divine will.[40]

Lesbian Feminist Theology

Heyward does offer some reflections on death and AIDS. In *Touching Our Strength* she states,

> Death is a passage – into what, we are not sure. But I am confident that the irrepressible love of God, the sacred power of the erotic, does not simply leave us behind at our death. An experience of undying friendship can provide the basis of an eschatology: of how we experience endings. Closure, termination, and death can be cruel and harsh, unjust and unwelcome. In friendship, however, the end is not final. Friends bear one another up here and now and well into eternity, the realm outside of time as we measure it.[41]

The power of the erotic does not die and for Heyward the AIDS quilt is an example and a symbol of friends bearing each other up into eternity. (The AIDS quilt, also known as the NAMES Project, was initiated by the gay rights activist Cleve Jones in 1987. Each panel of the quilt is the size of a grave and it now consists of over 44,000 panels.[42] The UK has its own quilt.) What exactly this 'bearing up' means is unclear. In her latest book Heyward offers some further reflections upon death but these were not prompted by AIDS but by the death of her beloved dog, Teraph. With Teraph Heyward experienced a relationship of erotic power, true mutuality and friendship and

> When Teraph died, I entered for a moment with him into that mysterious realm beyond the boundaries of human intelligence in which I caught a glimpse of the sacred truth that both he and I are participants in the life of God, and will be forever.[43]

What being a participant in the life of God beyond death, as opposed to before death, involves is never explained. In her earlier work, *Speaking of Christ*, reflecting on her experiences in Nicaragua, Heyward reveals that she has learned that 'the living' include the dead who have worked for the well being of humanity. At the funerals of those killed by the Contras the names of the dead would be read and the people would respond 'Presente!' They were summoning back the dead and testifying to the fact that they were in fact not gone at all. Heyward believes that this is the same sense in which Jesus is still alive. The dead are 'members of a Body that cannot be buried and forgotten',[44] this is the body of Christ incarnate in specific communities. In a sermon for All Saints Day in the same volume Heyward declares, 'I believe in heaven. I believe that those who have died are with us now. I have come to believe that the place to find and get in touch with the saints is wherever we are right now …'.[45] But these ideas are not fleshed out. Heyward does offer one paragraph of reflection upon death and AIDS. She seems to affirm belief in some sort of life beyond death (and this is born out in other reflections unconnected to AIDS) but what that might mean for the dead is unclear. The implications for the living are that they have a resource, a friendship to draw upon in their continuing struggle against injustice.

Hunt offers some reflections similar to but even briefer than Heyward's and these are not related to AIDS. Writing of a friend's conviction that she still felt in some sort of relationship with a departed friend Hunt reflects, 'This must be what eternal life is about … Maybe the so-called communion of saints are our old friends. Why not? I cannot imagine a better definition'.[46]

Melanie May is a lesbian feminist theologian who has endeavoured to construct a body theology out of her experience part of which was an experience of serious illness. She describes this theology as a 'theo-poetics of death and resurrection'. In her experience death and resurrection are not events that come at the end and beyond the end of a person's life but the pattern and practice of Christian living.[47] Death is a letting go of disconnection, of wrong relationship, resurrection is to experience connection, that is, right relationship. These reflections are prompted by May's own experiences not by AIDS.

In *Just Good Friends* Stuart offers a short reflection upon the fact that AIDS has convinced her of the unity of soul and body and therefore that 'only bodily resurrection is a good enough hope for these people'.[48] She sees that hope reflected powerfully in the final scene of Norman René's 1990 film *Long-Time Companion*:

> The surviving characters find themselves on the beach on a sunny day, greeting all their departed friends who have shed their emaciated, scarred bodies and stand tall, filled out, healthy, beautiful. They laugh together, hug each other, play together. If we believe in a God of justice, a God of love, a God of incarnation, this is the only possible ending: re-embodiment, re-incarnation. What form that might take I have no idea: whether it be in returning to and becoming again part of the body of the earth, or in the assumption of a different kind of body in a different dimension, such as Paul Imagined (1Corinthians 15.35–55), or some other speculative theory which is not grounded in a dualistic understanding of the human person.[49]

In a book on sainthood written a year after *Just Good Friends* Stuart concludes with two possible feminist theologies of sainthood. The first which she labels 'the minimalist approach' is one in which saints 'live' in the memory of others, their example inspiring and challenging down the centuries and across the miles. The second approach Stuart labels 'a daring theology of sainthood' in which she seeks to construct a theology of life after death whilst taking into account the feminist theological belief that the search for immortality is a peculiar quest of the male ego that has contributed towards eco-destruction. Stuart combines Rosemary Radford Ruether's notion that human beings, like all matter, decay and are 'composed back into the nexus of matter to rise again as new organic forms'[50] and the common feminist theological notion that the earth is God's body to suggest that 'those who have died continue to nourish and sustain their community from the heart of the body of God which has received them. Their energy, their thirst for justice warms and nourishes the roots of their community like compost around a plant'.[51] In the sacred space of imagination and play this energy can be re-membered and put together again as individual persons. In this book Stuart does at least attempt to construct some theology of the afterlife but it is a construction unrelated to AIDS and the issues it raises.

In an essay written a year after the book on saints and directly inspired by Vasey's work Stuart argues that gay and lesbian theology must recover an eschatological space because it must be true to its nature as a theology of hope and because an eschatological space is a space 'beyond' contemporary discourse, a space to think the unthinkable, a space in which the imagination flourishes. This is the space, for example, in which Jesus declared that marriage and family life had no ultimate value by teaching that there would be no marriage in heaven, 'of course, any talk about life after death ... tells us nothing about life after death ... but ... a great deal about our current values and aspirations'.[52] AIDS had inspired some very moving images of 'life after':

> from a re-reading (or re-singing) of Judy Garland's 'Somewhere Over the Rainbow' as an anthem of pride and hope for life beyond the rainbow flag (a symbol of lesbian and gay liberation), which quickly became popular, to a re-singing of the Village People's classic, 'Go West', which was originally written as a celebration of the freedom for lesbian and gay people found on the west coast of the United States (rather naughtily borrowing the tune from a Christian chorus). But in the shadow of AIDS it became a vision of life beyond the virus and dis-ease (*sic*), a life of solidarity and mutuality, of teaching and learning and of basking in the glory of the sun.[53]

And all these images of 'life after' testify to the ultimate value of embodiment, relationship and community. The AIDS quilt also demonstrates that people understand themselves in a communal context. Thus Stuart suggests 'communities of resistance create eschatological visions of "life after" in order to provide some common content to the hope and struggle for liberation'.[54] In Stuart and Heyward and minimally in Hunt we see theologians who are at some level conscious of the fact that AIDS does raise issues about life after death but they are incapable of actually talking about life after death except as a way of talking about now or in the vaguest manner. Here they demonstrate themselves to be under the tyranny of two forces the first is the 'orthodoxy' of eco-feminist theology that proclaims that the search for immortality is a distinctly patriarchal trait and the second is the rationalism of modernity that has constricted and suffocated the theological imagination and dis-enchanted our lives. Thus enslaved they are prevented from responding to the experience they make foundational to their theology. But at least these theologians attempted to address the issue of death and the afterlife in the shadow of AIDS. Other lesbian feminist theologians have not – Gilson says nothing at all on the subject and Mollenkott simply reprises Heyward's reflections on the quilt commenting that 'the yearning tenderness of the AIDS quilt panels certainly provides evidence from contemporary experience of the interconnection between spirituality and sexuality, ultimacy and intimacy'.[55]

Paralysis and Repetition

It is staggering how little AIDS impacted upon gay and lesbian theology written in the 1980s and early to mid 1990s. Its impact is evident mainly in discussion of sexual ethics. The fact that thousands of gay men were facing issues around mortality, including issues of life after death, seems to have by-passed some gay and lesbian theologians altogether and impinged upon the consciousness of some who struggle with how to deal with it. It is here that we can see the intellectual constraints put upon gay and lesbian theology by its construction within liberal and liberationist theological models. Liberal theology with its debt to Enlightenment rationalism has always tended to emphasise the symbolic nature of doctrine, adopted strategies of demythologisation and has therefore tended to collapse eschatology into ethics. Feminist theology has tended to be virulently opposed to any notion of an afterlife. Rosemary Radford Ruether has argued that,

By pretending that we can immortalise ourselves, our souls, and perhaps even our bodies for some future resurrection, we are immortalising our garbage and polluting the earth. If we are really to learn to recycle our garbage as fertilizer for new growth, our waste as matter for new artefacts, we need a spirituality of recycling that accepts ourselves as part of that process of growth, decay, reintegration into the earth and new growth.[56]

This position has been absorbed into much gay and lesbian theology as an 'orthodoxy' to be repeated as if obviously true. The prospect of becoming compost in the body of the divine may be an attractive one for people who are able to live long, nourished, largely healthy and fulfilled lives. None of the HIV+ men nor their supporters interviewed by Sollis cited this as their hope. Their hope tended to be much more traditional, focussed either on union with God, or reunion with others in the presence of God and/or bodily resurrection.[57] The repetition of 'orthodoxies' and the struggle with liberal/ liberationist traditions rendered gay and lesbian theology incapable of dealing with the profoundest theological questions raised by those living with HIV/ AIDS. It also isolated them from rich ingredients for theological reflection.

Sollis demonstrates that AIDS funerals, often designed by the deceased themselves, were usually 'defiant celebrations' or rather, performances, of gay identity in which that gay identity was played out in such an over-the-top camp style as to point to a reality beyond it. They also challenged the dominant construction of death as natural and non-tragic at the same time as defying the dominant construction of the gay/ HIV+ man as a tragic figure. Only McNeill shows any real grasp of the importance of the issues of mortality and life after death and here his liberalism cracks somewhat and his Catholicism takes over. Fortunato also, by recognising the limits of his liberalism and adopting a more postmodern approach, is able to acknowledge the importance of the issue and attempt to reflect upon it. Others like Heyward and Stuart also appear to feel the strain of their theological parameters but ultimately lose their nerve. They can only go so far and no further. Theologians are not the only gay and lesbian academics to have avoided these issues. Tim Edwards has observed the same reluctance to deal with issues surrounding dying in gay and lesbian studies.[58] He attributes this reluctance to a desire to avoid reinforcing the popular perception that AIDS is a disease that only impacts on gay people. Many gay and lesbian theologians argue that because of their status as non-reproducers gay people are associated in western society with death and AIDS has reinforced this connection. Perhaps some of these theologians were anxious not to further this perception by dealing with questions of death and the afterlife.

Whatever the reasons gay and lesbian theology largely failed to respond to the experiences of those living and dying with HIV/AIDS and thereby exposed the fragility of its own methodology and claim to authority. In the face of a reality that liberal and feminist theologies could not deal with, too many gay and lesbian theologians found themselves incapable of doing any more than repeating the 'orthodoxies' of these foundational theologies. Experience actually did not count nor was it not powerful enough to carry them further than these 'orthodoxies' and it is hard to imagine what could be more powerful for these theologians than the death of friends. McNeill is therefore to be admired for giving such prominence to the theology of death and the afterlife in his work. But there is a further aspect of the AIDS crisis, another sort of death, that McNeill has been incapable of dealing with and that is the death of the subject.

AIDS is both the symbol and the sacrament of post-modernity. It undermined the grand narratives of medicine and science, exposing their vulnerability and it also undermined the very concepts of identity and categories of being upon which gay and lesbian theology, even that which claims to be social constructionist, has been built. As Thomas Yingling has put it,

> the material effects of AIDS depleted so many of our cultural assumptions about identity, justice, desire, and knowledge that it seems at times able to threaten the entire system of Western thought – that which maintains the health and immunity of our epistemology: the psychic presence of AIDS signifies a collapse of identity and difference that refuses to be abjected from the systems of self-knowledge.[59]

AIDS challenged how we know ourselves. It challenged our categories of sexual identity and destabilised the modern subject. The failure to deal with this death is evident in McNeill's work in the repetition of his belief in the gay subject. This is also true in the work of other gay liberal and liberationist theologians. Heyward and Hunt make less of the lesbian subject and more of the female subject. These theologians, even those who are social constructionists, believe that there is some form of subjectivity stable enough to build a theology upon.

So much uncritical repetition signals that something is wrong, that there is a desire to make it so simply by saying it often enough, whether it is McNeill's belief in the authentic gay self, the lesbian feminist belief in the erotic and the patriarchal nature of life after death or Clark's belief in the redundancy of a 'rescuing' God, it creates an illusion of 'truth' and 'fact'. Jordan has drawn attention to repetition as a rhetorical device in Vatican documents on homosexuality. He argues that it is a way of creating the illusion of authority, stability and immutability whilst at the same time avoiding any challenges to it. It also involves a flattening out and consuming of history and/or experience.[60] The same process are evident in gay and lesbian theology. Constant repetition gives the impression of fact that is based in lesbian and gay experience, it does not create space for a counter voice. But the constant repetition in both cases is also a reaction against that which challenges it, there would not be a need for repetition otherwise. Many gay and lesbian theologians continue to assume and repeat the existence of a gay subject (even a socially constructed one) when AIDS highlighted the difficulties of classifying people according to sexual preferences, perhaps because this would be one grief too many to bear. But it is nevertheless a denial in the face of reality and once again a failure to be true to their own methodology and claims for authority.

Gay and lesbian theology stuttered, stumbled and crumbled over the graves of those lost to AIDS. Whilst there is evidence to suggest that those living with the virus and their supporters employed both theological resources, experience and their own imaginations in the face of death – even non-theologians have suggested that the AIDS quilt expresses an implicit belief in an afterlife[61] – those theologians who lives were most directly affected by AIDS appeared to have been paralysed by pre-existing theological paradigms and assumptions which they could only repeat.

Gay and lesbian theology has achieved much. It has given a theological voice to those who had been deprived of one and thus built for lesbian and gay Christians a room of their own, a place of safety from homophobic discourse and practice, a place to find God. It has exposed the heterosexist bias of much theology and deconstructed it. It has offered new paradigms for relating not just with other people but with the whole created world. But AIDS exposed its limits and its weaknesses. Although people still do gay and lesbian theology because they have not yet accepted and grieved the loss of the modern subject, gay and lesbian theology has been largely displaced and replaced by the emergence of queer theology and in the major work of Robert Goss we can detect the process of theological shift between these two theologies.

Notes

1   I gratefully acknowledge the important research done by David Sollis on this issue contained in his PhD thesis 'Queering Death: A Theological Analysis of the Reconnection of Desire and Immortality in the Shadow of AIDS', which has emerged from The Queering of Death research project I run at King Alfred's College, Winchester.
2   Vasey, *Strangers and Friends*, p. 240.
3   Vasey, *Strangers and Friends*, p. 243.
4   Vasey, *Strangers and Friends*, p. 245.
5   Vasey, *Strangers and Friends*, pp. 248–9.
6   Sollis, 'Queering Death', p. 110.
7   Sollis, 'Queering Death', p. 111.
8   Sollis, 'Queering Death', pp. 150–51.
9   Sollis, 'Queering Death', p. 155.
10 T. Anne Richards and Susan Folkman, 'Spiritual Aspects of Loss at the Time of a Partner's Death from AIDS', *Death Studies* 21 (February 1997), pp. 527–52.
11 http://www.avert.org/usastaty.htm.
12 http://www.phls.co.uk/facts/HIV/HivNewMen.htm.
13 Beth Schneider and Nancy Stoller, *Women Resisting AIDS* (Philadelphia: Temple University Press, 1995).
14 John E. Fortunato, *AIDS: The Spiritual Dilemma* (San Francisco: Harper and Row, 1987), p. 119.
15 McNeill, *Taking a Chance on God*, pp. 146–75.
16 John J. McNeill, 'The Gay Response to AIDS: Becoming a Resurrection People', *The Way* 28.4 (October 1988), p. 338.
17 McNeill, *Taking a Chance on God*, p. 153.
18 McNeill, *Freedom, Glorious Freedom*, pp. 61–71.
19 Chris Glaser, *Come Home! Reclaiming Spirituality and Community as Gay Men and Lesbians* (San Francisco: Harper and Row, 1990), p. 202.
20 Glaser, *Come Home!*, p. 206.
21 Glaser, *Come Home!*, p. 206.
22 Clark, *A Place to Start*, p. 48.
23 Clark, *A Place to Start*, p. 67.
24 Clark, *A Place to Start*, p. 75.
25 Clark, *A Place to Start*, p. 105.
26 Clark, *A Place to Start*, p. 107.
27 Clark, *A Place to Start*, p. 46.
28 Clark, *Beyond Our Ghettos*, p. 43.
29 Ronald E. Long, 'God Through Gay Men's Eyes: Gay Theology in the Age of AIDS', in R.E. Long and J.M. Clark (eds), *AIDS, God and Faith: Continuing the Dialogue* (Dallas: Monument Press, 1992), p. 18.

30 Kathleen M. Sands, *Escape from Paradise: Evil and Tragedy in Feminist Theology* (Minneapolis: Augsburg Fortress Press, 1994).
31 Clark, *Defying the Darkness*, p. 93.
32 Spencer, *Gay and Gaia*, pp. 345–7.
33 Comstock, *Gay Theology Without Apology*, pp. 1–5.
34 Cleaver, *Know My Name*, pp. 117 and 136.
35 Cleaver, *Know My Name*, pp. 112–37.
36 Cleaver, *Know My Name*, p. 137.
37 Cleaver, *Know My Name*, pp. 144–5.
38 Cleaver, *Know My Name*, p. 148.
39 Tim Morrison, 'Bodies, Sex, Wholeness and Death', in Stuart, *Religion is a Queer Thing*, pp. 122–3.
40 See for example, João Baptista Libânio, 'Hope, Utopia, Resurrection', in Jon Sobrino and Ignacio Ellacuría (eds), *Systematic Theology: Perspectives from Liberation Theology* (London: SCM, 1996), pp. 279–90.
41 Heyward, *Touching Our Strength*, p. 138.
42 Cleve Jones, *Stitching a Revolution: The Making of an Activist* (San Francisco: HarperSanFrancisco, 2000).
43 Heyward, *Saving Jesus From Those who are Right*, p. 75.
44 Heyward, *Speaking of Christ*, p. 27.
45 Heyward, *Speaking of Christ*, p. 62.
46 Hunt, *Fierce Tenderness*, p. 32.
47 Melanie May, *A Body Knows: A Theopoetics of Death and Resurrection* (New York: Continuum, 1995).
48 Stuart, *Just Good Friends*, p. 150.
49 Stuart, *Just Good Friends*, p. 150.
50 Rosemary Radford Ruether, 'Ecofeminism and Healing Ourselves, Healing the Earth', *Feminist Theology* 9 (May 1995), p. 61.
51 Elizabeth Stuart, *Spitting at Dragons: Towards a Feminist Theology of Sainthood* (London: Mowbray, 1996), p. 115.
52 Elizabeth Stuart, 'Sex in Heaven: The Queering of Theological Discourse on Sexuality', in Davies and Loughlin (eds), p. 195.
53 Stuart, 'Sex in Heaven', p. 196.
54 Stuart, 'Sex in Heaven', p. 204.
55 Mollenkott, *Sensuous Spirituality*, p. 105.
56 Rosemary Radford Ruether, 'Ecofeminism and Healing Ourselves, Healing the Earth', p. 61.
57 Sollis, 'Queering Death', pp. 101–79.
58 Tim Edwards, 'The AIDS Dialectics: Awareness, Identity, Death, and Sexual Politics', in Ken Plummer (ed.), *Modern Homosexualities: Fragments of Lesbian and Gay Experience* (London and New York: Routledge, 1992), p. 155.
59 Thomas Yingling, 'AIDS in America: Postmodern Governance, Identity, and Experience', in Diana Fuss (ed.), *Inside/Out: Lesbian Theories, Gay Theories* (New York and London: Routledge, 1991), p. 292.
60 Jordan, *The Silence of Sodom*, pp. 51–9.
61 Timothy Murphy and Suzanne Poirier (eds), *Writing AIDS: Gay Literature, Language and Analysis* (New York: Columbia University Press, 1997), p. 314.

Chapter 6

From Here to Queer

In 1993 Robert Goss, a former Jesuit priest and gay/AIDS activist published *Jesus Acted Up: A Gay and Lesbian Manifesto*. This book is significant in the history of gay and lesbian theology because it marks the transition from gay and lesbian theology to queer theology. This book never completely tips into through-going queer theology but it lays the groundwork for it to develop.

Foregrounding Foucault

Although other gay and lesbian theologians like Heyward and Stuart had referred to and drawn upon the work of Foucault, Goss was the first to centre Foucault's theory and methodology in the process of doing theology. Goss isolates four particular aspects of Foucault's thought which form the basis of the theology outlined in his book. The first is Foucault's theory that power flows through society through discourse, a historically and culturally conditioned way of speaking and writing which determines what a particular culture 'knows' to be right and desirable. The second is Foucault's distinctive genealogical method which analyses the flow of power in social discourse and practice, not simply the power of rule but the power of resistance to that rule which is always present. The purpose of this method is to summon up the 'subjugated knowledges' contained in this resistance and use them to deconstruct the dominant discourse, revealing its limitations and hidden assumptions. Goss wants to apply this genealogical method to

> Christological discursive practices that have subsumed Jesus into abstract formulations of heterosexist values and ideas. I also include the production of biblical truth as heterosexist truth. My application of genealogical method intends to recover the dangerous memories of Jesus and biblical truth from their captivity within a heterosexist system of discursive practice. Christology is liberated from a pseudouuniversal discursive practice and recontextualised to the experience of gay and lesbian people. Likewise the Bible is rescued from fundamentalism and becomes an empowering resource for gay/lesbian resistance.[1]

Goss also wants to draw upon the reverse discourse of resistance developed by gay and lesbian people since the Stonewall Riots which unmasks the universal claims of heterosexual discourse and exposes the exclusion of gay and lesbian people from its claims. The third aspect of Foucault's thought that Goss uses is Foucault's analysis of power and its relation to knowledge. For Foucault power is not a property to be held by a dominant elite but a complex matrix of strategies and techniques present everywhere. Knowledge is the use of power in the development and maintenance of discourse. Knowledge which becomes dominant is 'truth' and there is a constant battle in any society over the production of truth which is in essence a battle for power. Discourses can be displaced and replaced by other discourses. So homophobic discourse can be challenged, deconstructed and replaced by an alternative discourse that emerges out of gay and lesbian resistance to homophobic discourse. Finally, Goss utilises Foucault's theory of the social construction of sexuality. Foucault famously asserted that, 'sexuality must not be understood as a stubborn drive, by nature alien and of necessity disobedient to a power which exhausts itself trying to subdue it and often fails to control it entirely. It appears rather as an especially dense transfer point for relations of power'.[2] Sexuality is a discourse within which bodies are regulated. The modern concept of sexual identity was the result of the medicalisation of sexual discourse Thus a universal history of lesbian and gay people is simply not possible because same-sex sexual acts have been configured in different ways in cultural discourses across the centuries.

'Queering' the Pitch

Goss therefore sets out to develop a gay and lesbian liberation theology grounded in Foucauldian methodology. This type of theology will involve a critical analysis of the social location and discursive practices that gay and lesbian people find themselves enmeshed within as well as gay/lesbian discourse with a view to inaugurating political change: 'a gay/lesbian liberation theology begins with resistance and moves to political insurrection'.[3] But Goss also describes his theology as a 'queer' theology. He uses the term queer here in the activist sense which developed in the AIDS crisis to refer to the coalitions formed between lesbians, gay men and feminist women, 'queer is a term of political dissidence and sexual difference'.[4] It is out of his experience of queer activism that Goss writes.

Goss begins his book with a genealogical analysis of the social organisation of homophobia from heterosexist socialisation through stereotyping and the development of a language of deviance through the medicalisation of homosexuality in the nineteenth century which created the homosexual as both criminally deviant and psychologically and physically sick, to the Christian discourses on sexuality that construct heterosexuality as God's will and homosexuality as a violation of that will. Goss also analyses the institutionalisation of homophobia from the education system that presumes all children are heterosexual and reinforces rigid gender roles, to the hounding of gay and lesbian personnel from the military, to the deprivation of basic civil rights to lesbian and gay people. Goss notes that it was only once AIDS began to effect the 'general population' of the USA that the government began to take much interest or spend much money on the problem. AIDS was constructed as a gay disease and used to further reinforced homophobic discourses the result of which was an increase in anti gay/lesbian violence. Homophobia is a form of social control designed to keep lesbian and gay people in their closets and protect the privileged status of heterosexuality.

Goss goes on to chart (summarising Foucault) how the medicalisation of homophobia not only created a new species of person but also created a reverse discourse of resistance among that very people. It enabled gay and lesbian people to find each other, articulate a public voice and to forge a cultural identity. Greater persecution only increased the visibility of lesbian and gay people enabling them to form more and larger support groups until the Stonewall Riots precipitated the end of the tactics of assimilation and the era of 'gay power'. Coming out became the means by which a gay/lesbian identity was produced, tested and affirmed in community and a gay/lesbian identity was now understood as a political act resisting and challenging the structures of heterosexism and homophobia. Transgressive action became the order of the day in the immediate aftermath of Stonewall and though reformist activism continued to exist and began to dominate in the late 1970s, early 1980s the advent of AIDS revived the practice of transgressive action in the shape of such organisations as Queer Nation, ACT UP (AIDS Coalition to Unleash Power) or the Sisters of Perpetual Indulgence (or OUTRAGE! and the Lesbian Avengers in the UK). Transgressive activists positively flaunt their cultural distinctiveness. They seek to destabilise the dominant discourses by acting out their stereotypes, parodying gender stereotypes, interrupting events, engaging in non-violent direct action, sometimes 'outing' those in positions of public influence and power who have supported homophobic structures or actions. The Sisters of Perpetual Indulgence, for example, are an international 'organisation' of gay male nuns who seek to rid the world of guilt around sexuality and encourage safe sex. They declare prominent gay activists saints (in the UK the late artist and film director Derek Jarman and theologians Elizabeth Stuart and Bernard Lynch are among those who have been canonised) and generally act out a reverse of the discourse of contemporary Roman Catholicism around homosexuality. ACT UP fought against an institutional indifference to HIV/AIDS by invading and picketing. Perhaps most famously ACT UP interrupted a mass at St Patrick's Cathedral, New York in protest against Cardinal O'Connor's anti-gay and anti-safe sex activities.

Foucault realised that a gay/lesbian identity was not given it was made and that therefore it was possible to imagine and work towards new ways of relating, new forms of language and truth, new forms of love and pleasure. If lesbian and gay people were conscious of the constructed nature of their identity then they could choose to reconstruct their identities in ways that escaped the worst of heterosexual society and this is what Goss wants lesbian and gay theologians to do.

The Queer Christ

Goss maintains that Christology has been used to convey an anti-sexual rhetoric throughout Christian history. Distrust of sexual pleasure, desire and the body were absorbed into Christian discourse through the influence of Hellenistic philosophy and Gnosticism. The doctrine of the Virgin Birth and the construction of Jesus as a celibate both reflected and reinforced the Church's increasing distrust of the sexual and its promotion of the 'ascetic self'. Jesus' asexual maleness became normative and divinised with the result that women were excluded from full participation in the Church. Though the Reformation brought a change of emphasis the result was equally unfortunate with heterosexual marriage and family life now occupying the pedestal upon which the idol of celibacy had sat. Even contemporary Roman Catholicism worships this new idol.

Having deconstructed traditional Christology Goss sets out to develop a queer Christology. He roots his Christology in Jesus' proclamation of the *basileia*, the reign of God which 'signified the political transformation of his society into a radically egalitarian, new age, where sexual, social, religious, and political distinctions would be irrelevant'.[5] Jesus acted out his *basileia* message by standing with the oppressed and the outcast of his society and by forming a discipleship of equals. In a social structure in which Jewish peasants were crippled by debt Jesus proclaimed a God who cancelled debt and offered not only daily bread but also feasts. This was politically explosive and led Jesus to the cross. The key event that led to Jesus' death was what Goss labels the Stop the Temple action which was Jesus' most transgressive demonstration of the 'egalitarian, unbrokered reign of God'.[6]

Goss argues that at Easter Jesus became the queer Christ. This is not any comment upon Jesus' sexuality, although Goss is keen to point out the homophobic assumptions that lie behind the construction of an asexual or heterosexual Christ. Rather, for Goss the resurrection is God's 'coming out' on the side of Jesus, confirming his *basileia* message. Jesus' resurrection is therefore the hope for queer people for it is through it that God turns Jesus into a parable about God and so we know that God is on the side of the oppressed. At Easter 'God raised Jesus to the level of a discursive symbol and praxis, and Jesus became the Christ, the liberative praxis of God's compassion in the world'.[7] So that for all time and space Jesus stands in solidarity with the oppressed. Just as it possible for black people to proclaim that 'Jesus is black' and women to relate to the image of the Christa, so it is that queer people can declare that 'Jesus is queer'. Indeed, if Jesus is not queer then the gospel is at best irrelevant and at worst bad news for queer people.

Queering the Bible

Following feminist and liberation biblical hermeneutics Goss seeks to develop a hermeneutics based upon the epistemological privilege of the oppressed and a hermeneutics of suspicion. He seeks to deconstruct the 'texts of terror' that have been used to inspire and condone homophobic violence – the story of Sodom and Gomorrah which is a story about rape and the blatant infringement of the ancient codes of hospitality, the Levitical and Deuteronomic texts which Goss argues are actually aimed against male cultic prostitution, I Corinthians 6.9 which, following Boswell, Goss argues refers to male prostitutes, Jude 7 and 2 Peter 2.10 which are actually about the violation of the natural order by lust for angels and Romans 1.26–27 which assumes a derivation from nature due to idolatry. Goss' point is that the 'obvious' references to homosexuality in these passages are not in fact obvious at all but constructed. Biblical 'truth' has been produced in the context of power relations, queer Christians are now reading the Bible for themselves and producing their own truth. This is the truth of a God who consistently sides with the oppressed, who is working to bring about justice and who promises a just society for everyone. To produce such a truth we need queer theologians and publishers who are prepared to read the Bible as their own and intertextually with their own resistance to oppression. So the lives of queer people become a text in dialogue with the biblical text:

> Through a hermeneutics of solidarity, queer Christians can stand with the band of fugitive Israelite slaves that escaped Egyptian oppression, with the heroes and heroines of Hebrew scriptures, the hopes of liberation of the conquered Jewish people, and the liberated hopes

of the nascent Jesus movement against the background of Jewish nationalism and Roman politics of domination.[8]

Furthermore, reading their own struggles through a hermeneutic of solidarity encourages queer Christians to remember Jesus' *basileia* practice and to imitate it, engaging in solidarity, compassion, loving service, transgressive action and inclusive table fellowship with others who are oppressed.

Goss gives an example of a queer hermeneutic in his reading of the exorcism narratives in Mark. Goss argues that behaviour commonly diagnosed as mental illness is often an expression of resistance to oppressive political forces but society by labelling people who manifest these forms of resistance 'mentally ill' seeks to neutralise their protest. The exorcism stories are about Jesus' confrontation with oppressive political forces. Like the boy in Mark 9.14–24 gay and lesbian people have often been rendered dumb by the Church and also classified as ill and/or deviant. They have been made into the demonised other. Jesus through his exorcisms confronted and disrupted the forces of oppression in his society and their impact upon people, for something is truly demonic when it stands against the *basileia* and this is exactly what homophobia does. The queer Christ is then one who fights for queer people dominated by homophobia, he confronts and overthrows the social forces that prevent queer people from knowing themselves as free.

This is the nature of queer theology – liberation. Doctrines are only of use to queer Christians in so far as they can be practiced for liberation. Queer Christians are not interested in abstract, universal doctrines because they are in the midst of a political struggle for their lives. The gospels provide queer Christians with the dangerous memory of a subjugated knowledge of a God who stands in solidarity with the oppressed, a God who stands with the thousands of gay men and lesbians killed in the Holocaust, the millions of people who have been persecuted, tortured and killed for loving members of the same sex through history, the thousands of men who have died with AIDS and the victims of hate crimes, 'God will remember them and do justice'.[9]

Embracing the Exile (again)

Queer Christians are called not just to remember Jesus' *basileia* practice but also to imitate it. For Goss, this means, among other things, interrogating ourselves closely if we chose to remain within our churches. Such a decision can only be justified if we engage in open and active challenges to Christian homophobic discourse. Goss thinks that to embrace the exile is to act with more integrity and is a better witness to the *basileia* because in the exile queer Christians can create an alternative social and ecclesial space in which to attempt to build a community of *basileia* practice, a non-hierarchical discipleship of equals which operates through consensus and is proactive in seeking to expose and challenge ecclesial homophobia. He calls for the creation of 'hundreds and thousand of gay/lesbian-affirming base communities of faith that practice God's justice'.[10] In such communities preaching will be a communal, mutual activity in which 'queer biblical truth' is produced and circulated. It is a subversive and dangerous practice because it invokes and activates Jesus' *basileia* practice. In these communities *basileia* actions are symbolically represented in the sacraments, making it present in our midst. Church sacraments frequently exclude or marginalize lesbian and gay bodies. Baptism and confirmation can either be reappropriated or discarded for new rituals which embody the initiation of queer Christians 'within a liminal community of companionship'[11] and into the struggle of *basileia* resistance. For queer people of course coming out is also part of this process and coming out needs to be ritualised. Queer Christian communities also need to recover the original power of the Eucharist which Goss describes as 'table companionship around a shared meal [which] is the location where the Bible and politics, God and society, faith and erotic practice interact'.[12] As a celebration of how God makes insiders of outsiders, it becomes for queer Christians an act of defiance against oppression. Queer Christians must also acknowledge their need for healing and reconciliation. In the shadow of AIDS the queer community has become the suffering servant of Isaiah, a community of pain and suffering but also a community of love-making and justice and this is clearly represented in the AIDS quilt. Unions between same-sex couples must be celebrated in these places in defiance of those Christians who dismiss their validity because they are 'sterile'. As 'gratuitous celebrations of love' usually much more equal, mutual and careful than heterosexual marriages, such unions become models of Christian love. In queer ecclesial communities ministers facilitate community through service to that community leading by example. In these communities then Goss envisages queer Christians taking back those things the Church has snatched from them and using them to produce a reverse community which exposes and challenges the oppressive nature of the Church. They will be visible signs of the failure of the Churches.

Transgressing

For Goss Jesus is a model of transgressive practice. His Stop the Temple action was the model for ACT UP's Stop the Church action. In the course of that action one protestor took communion and crumbled the communion wafer causing an almighty outcry in the media which labelled the action sacrilegious. Goss points out that whatever the wisdom of the action it was designed to draw attention to Cardinal O'Connor's sacrilegious disregard for the humanity and well-being of gay and lesbian people. Jesus too was accused of blasphemy, conflict is unavoidable for those committed to God's *basileia* practice. Queer Christians are called to act out God's reign in transgressive action, taking God into homophobic space to destroy it.

Essential to successful transgressive action is a spirit of self-criticism. Queer Christians needs to be wary of a tendency among oppressed groups to express internalised homophobia in hostility towards itself. Gay men are often sexist, lesbians and gay men can often be extremely hostile to heterosexual, bisexual and transgendered people, they can also be ageist, racist, classist and hostile to disabled people. Queer communities have to work on their own weaknesses as well as their oppression.

Theology

Finally Goss turns his attention to God who 'has to be liberated from ecclesial practice'.[13] God must be rescued from the pleasure denying, anti-sexual and masculinist tradition. For Goss this means following Heyward in re-visioning God as erotic power:

> God's erotic power bursts forth on Easter into connectedness or solidarity with the once-dead and now-risen Jesus. God's erotic power is revealed as a shared power with Jesus. In turn, Jesus the Christ becomes the sign of God's erotic power, breaking the linkages of erotic desire and inequality, and Easter becomes the mutual event of heart-connectedness ... . For queer Christians, erotic power is God's empowering way of acting in the world. It is God's way of saying that they are graced as lesbian women and gay men.[14]

Gay men and lesbians therefore name God as the 'coempowering ground of their erotic practice and spirituality'. This erotic power propels queer Christians into solidarity and connectedness with all other oppressed groups and with the earth itself. Practicing solidarity is essential to end the cycle of oppression. Queer faith practice, prayer, liturgy and transgressive action embodies erotic power. It is time, Goss believes, for queer Christians to lay hold of this erotic power and to start acting up, to take their holy anger into sacred space as Jesus did and as ACT UP and other groups have done. Queer Christians have been called to be prophets of God's reign confident that God will always have the final word.

So Queer and Yet So Far

No other work of gay and lesbian theology is quite as activist orientated as *Jesus Acted Up*. It is as the subtitle states a manifesto and ends with the rallying cry ACT UP! FIGHT BACK! END HATE![15] It is an exciting call to transgressive action in the name of the queer Christ. It is essentially a liberation theology but unlike most gay liberation theology is closer in the manner of its theological reflection to Latin American liberation theology than to process or feminist theology. Christ is absolutely central to Goss' theology and not the demythologised Christ of liberal theology or feminist theology but the resurrected Christ. Goss never attempts to demythologise the resurrection because he understands the resurrection to be the foundation of all and any hope for justice. And although Goss follows so many gay liberal and liberationist theologians in commending the exile, for him the exile is not the place in which to abandon Christian doctrine and practice but the place in which to appropriate and renew it. Foucault taught Goss that discourses cannot just be swept aside because they are all that we have, but they can be deconstructed, reversed and mined for subjugated knowledges. Goss therefore shows a much greater respect for and engagement with the Christian tradition than most other gay and lesbian theologians. In some places he does succumb to the gay and lesbian theological tendency to flatten out and caricature the tradition, for example in his conviction that the early Church became universally anti-sexual, thus cutting himself off from some useful subjugated discourses. He also occasionally falls into the repetition of gay and lesbian theological orthodoxies, for example, in his adoption of Heyward's understanding of the erotic which jars with his otherwise resolute refusal to make generalisations about lesbian and gay experience apart from the experience of oppression. Despite paying close attention to the AIDS crisis Goss has nothing to say in this book about the relation of the resurrection hope which he so passionately proclaims to the deaths of thousands of gay men. However, in a later essay written after the death of his partner, Frank, to AIDS Goss does address issues of grief and mourning. Queering the story of the relationship between Jesus and the Beloved Disciple and reading it as a relationship of sexual intimacy he tells the story of his partner's death through that biblical story. Goss notes,

> in grieving over physical absence, we often discover presence – identifying it with the energy and love, traditionally designated as the spirit that was the deceased. We continue a familial and loving bond with the deceased .... There is no loss of love in physical separation; in fact, there may be an increase of love as the continuing relationship moves from grief to solace .... I look forward to the day when death will die, when there will be no need for justice, and when all beloved disciples, lovers and Christ are reunited in an erotic dance of joy and communion.[16]

So Goss' theology in *Jesus Acted Up* seems to have laid the groundwork for some serious reflection on death and resurrection even though it itself does not address the issue with regard to AIDS. Interestingly, in the same volume of essays, most of which adopt the methodology of *Jesus Acted Up*, Jim Mitulski reads the book of Ezekiel through the lens of a people devastated by HIV/AIDS. He argues that it was Ezekiel's acquaintance with grief and suffering that gave him the credibility to speak about resurrection, 'perhaps it takes a prophet with AIDS to see the hope offered by a God with AIDS to a people whose survival depends on their ability to see through the lies told to us and by us'.[17] Like Ezekiel the gay community cannot marshall its strength until it has hope. Ezekiel saw the dry bones live, thousands of thousands of bones enfleshed. In the enormity of its loss the gay community cannot remember everyone who has been lost but God will remember. So Goss' work seems to have inspired some theological reflection on death and the afterlife.

Perhaps most puzzling of all for a theologian so indebted to Foucault is Goss's failure to reflect theologically on the production of identity. Though he acknowledges that gay and lesbian identities are social constructs he fails to interrogate their usefulness as theological categories and rather carries on as if they are stable identities. Since the social construction of identity is at the heart of Foucault's theory it is odd that Goss did not centralise it in his theology. His use of the term 'queer' may give the superficial impression that he has taken on board the full implications of a Foucauldian approach but in fact he uses the term as a short hand for gay and lesbians acting in transgressive coalitions.

Despite these weaknesses *Jesus Acted Up* remains a watershed in gay and lesbian theology for even though he did not follow Foucault's theory all the way through in this book, Goss nevertheless flagged up the issues of discourse and identity. Goss also demonstrated that a commitment to radical political action and a feminist and sex-positive theology did not have to involve a sweeping dismissal of the tradition, for the tradition is all we have to work with and read against the grain of heterosexist and homophobic interpretation can be good news for Christian queers. In short Goss proved that it was possible to still do theology and be committed to gay and lesbian liberation. His own credentials were impeccable on this score. As a member of ACT UP and Queer Nation he had been arrested on demonstrations and other actions. And more, Goss suggested, albeit only by implication, that theology could have something to teach the wider queer movement about hope, solidarity and justice.

Jesus Acted Up contains at some point within its pages all the flaws of gay liberal, liberationist and lesbian feminist theology, it too fails the AIDS test but there is something substantially different about its methodology. It itself is not a queer theology because it still leaves the categories of lesbian and gay and male and female in place and theologically unexamined but it paves the way for a thoroughgoing queer theology to emerge which changes everything.

Notes

1   Goss, *Jesus Acted Up*, p. 183.
2   Foucault, *The History of Sexuality, Volume 1*, p. 103.
3   Goss, *Jesus Acted Up*, p. xvii.
4   Goss, *Jesus Acted Up*, p. xix.
5   Goss, *Jesus Acted Up*, p. 73.
6   Goss, *Jesus Acted Up*, pp. 76–7.
7   Goss, *Jesus Acted Up*, p. 78.
8   Goss, *Jesus Acted Up*, p. 105.
9   Goss, *Jesus Acted Up*, p. 111.
10 Goss, *Jesus Acted Up*, p. 124.
11 Goss, *Jesus Acted Up*, p. 129.
12 Goss, *Jesus Acted Up*, p. 132.
13 Goss, *Jesus Acted Up*, p. 161.
14 Goss, *Jesus Acted Up*, p. 169.
15 Goss, *Jesus Acted Up*, p. 180.
16 Robert E. Goss, 'The Beloved Disciple: A Queer Bereavement Narrative in a Time of AIDS', in Robert E. Goss and Mona West (eds), *Take Back the Word: A Queer Reading of the Bible* (Cleveland: The Pilgrim Press, 2000), pp. 215–17.
17 Jim Mitulski, 'Ezekiel Understands AIDS: AIDS Understands Ezekiel or Reading the Bible with HIV', in Goss and West (eds), *Take Back the Word*, pp. 155–6.

Chapter 7

Queer Theology

Queer theology is still in its infancy and yet from the little that has been written it is clear that queer theology is radically different from gay and lesbian theology. This is because queer theorists, unlike gay liberationists, do not fight for the liberation of oppressed sexuality, their rallying cry is not to 'come out', rather their goal is to liberate everyone from contemporary constructions of sexuality (Foucault) and gender (Butler). For Butler this liberation can be brought about by practices that became known as 'gender fucking', performing the scripts of maleness and femaleness subversively. She believes that we cannot stand completely outside of those scripts but we can tinker with them in such a way as to reveal their non-essential and performative nature. Foucault looked for a slightly different escape route from Enlightenment constructions of the human person and found it in the pre-modern Christian ascetic self which was under constant self-scrutiny, conscious of being a self in production and which sought to de-sexualise the itself. Foucault also picked up from the Christian tradition a valorisation of male friendship. He came to believe that homosexuality was of value because of the relational possibilities – new and old – that it created. As Mark Vernon has noted for Foucault,

> Friendship is strategically important because it opens up new spaces for affection, tenderness, fidelity, camaraderie and companionship and so reveals the emotional emptiness of the tyranny of sexuality. Foucault illustrates how male homosexuality can be treated as an opportunity, an historic occasion to form new ways of being together.[1]

For Foucault to be gay was not to have a sexual identity characterised by certain psychological traits and ways of behaving, to be gay was to seek to develop a different type of life and way of relating to that demanded by the dominant discourses. In his project Foucault felt a strong affinity with early Christians particularly the monastic fathers.

Queer theory, then, questions the very notion of sexual identity. Although a significant number of gay and lesbian theologians have now embraced the essence of queer theory, so have a number of theologians who have not been identified with gay and lesbian theology and who identify as heterosexual or in a typically queer fashion do not buy into sexual categorisation at all. Queer theology is not an identity-based theology, indeed it is an anti-identity based theology. Queer theology is not a 'natural' development of gay and lesbian theology but rather an unnatural development which emerges from the fissures within gay and lesbian theology which the repetitions within it draw attention to. Yet, recalling that in French répétition has the meaning of rehearsal, it is true that queer theory and, to a large extent, queer theology have emerged from the rubble of gay and lesbian theory/theology. The performance of lesbian and gay identity did not prove to be terribly convincing theoretically or theologically.

Strangers and Friends

One of the earliest works of queer theology was Vasey's *Strangers and Friends*. Although Vasey does not explicitly engage with queer theory and mentions Foucault only in passing he nevertheless develops a distinctively queer approach to sexuality in this apologetic work aimed at fellow evangelicals. Vasey's methodology is genealogical. He regards male same-sex desire (he has nothing to say about female desire) as a cultural phenomenon, configured, practiced and interpreted differently in different cultural contexts. Like Foucault he draws attention to the consistent valorisation of male same-sex friendship in the Christian tradition and the social and theological recognition of friendship in the works of monks such as Aelred of Rievaulx or the liturgical rites of 'making of brothers' uncovered by John Boswell. Alongside this he traces the emergence of the sin of sodomy from the ranks of 'ordinary' sins to something particularly frightening that had to be punished and destroyed. This development, which seems to have occurred from the thirteenth century, was probably the result of many factors such as the association of same-sex behaviour with the extravagant aristocracy at the time when the urban merchant class with its small households was emerging and the strenuous effort to enforce clerical celibacy. The sodomite was constructed as a vile creature whose very existence destabilised the human and divine orders. The myth of the sodomite still holds some sway in the western imagination today. Yet even as the sodomite was being produced and reviled Shakespeare could celebrate men's affection and explore themes of androgyny and gender performance in his plays. In the late seventeenth century a new form of homosexuality emerged in England as the rising middle class, individualism, and the notion of companionate marriage, which established a distinctive pattern of gender roles, led to a suspicion of passionate male friendships and the forming of a new identity for those who wished to hold on to them:

> The pattern of homosexuality that emerged at the beginning of the eighteenth century can be summarised as follows. A social identity arises that both borrows the gender categories of the culture and also provides an ironic critique of them. It provides a cultural counterpoint to the domestic ideal fostered by the economic arrangements in society.[2]

The nineteenth century saw the development of the free market which constructed social relationships around competition. The competitive element in male relationships was emphasised, as were virtues of self-reliance and discipline. Work was relocated away from the home and the domestic sphere and femininity became associated with passivity and emotion. The family became the refuge from the public sphere of competition. At the same time the free market emphasised the importance of free choice and the moral neutrality of the market place created a place for gay men to exercise that free choice in forming a culture as long as they could afford to do so. Science also claimed the right to interpret the world in the nineteenth century and it turned homosexuality from a sin, crime and deviance into a personality type which could be categorised, studied and controlled. Science gave gay people a name, an identity and an ambiguous place in society as sick rather than evil which the gay liberation movement took and subverted. Vasey points out to those Christians who bemoan the existence of gay people and a gay subculture that in absorbing and baptising modernity's constructions of the family, masculinity and femininity, Christians and particularly the Protestant Churches, created the very context out of which modern western homosexuality emerged. Indeed, Vasey accuses his fellow evangelicals of idolising modern social order with the result they have to bear responsibility for what he considers to be the most serious consequence of the modern social order which is the diversion 'of the human instinct for worship from God and the city of God – to use St Augustine's phrase – and redirect it towards the sexual attraction between men and women'.[3] Gay men can be understood as noble resisters of this idolatry and 'those who find themselves the enemy of idols cannot be very far from the mysterious presence of the true and living God'.[4]

For Vasey Genesis teaches that nature waits for humanity to bring it to perfection. Though it is tainted by sin human culture is humanity's attempt to ever live out and up to that vocation. In that sense we are little gods with enormous freedom but ever called to discern the mind of God in our creativity. The scriptures also teach us that we are not merely or even primarily individuals but part of social units. These two theological insights come together in the Christian task of discerning the scriptures, it must always be a corporate task, it must exclude no one, it must recognise the cultural contextuality of scripture and it must acknowledge that wisdom exists beyond the Church. Vasey points out that both the Old and New Testament discourses on sexuality reveal something very important, first that these ancient communities *included* people who engaged in a variety of sexual practices and second that their communities were able to discuss these matter openly and, for St Paul, not in the context of blind obedience but in the context of grace – God's own loving acceptance which itself generates goodness and which is expressed most clearly and perfectly in Jesus. Jesus is 'the shape of grace' and Jesus' life was characterised by the friendships he formed, the friendships with sinners and the friendship with disciples. Vasey suggests that gay people may have a role to play in reminding and recalling the Church to friendship which up until modernity was a major theme of the Christian faith. Any discernment of scripture must take place in the context of a Church which welcomes gay people because embracing the outsider is the shape of grace. Vasey is also insistent that any discussion on homosexuality in the Church has to take place with the realisation that homosexuality is always a cultural phenomenon.

> In the cultural environment that shaped these texts, the public face of homosexuality was the hungry, idolatrous assertiveness of 'normal' masculinity ... . The emergence of a public gay identity since the eighteenth century has created a very different situation. The public face of homosexuality is now associated with those who – for whatever reason – find themselves unable to accommodate to the robust 'heterosexual' masculinity of the culture, to the suppression of public affection outside the home, and to the culture's identification of desire and 'heterosexual' domesticity. Modern gay identity, on this reading, is not proud rebellion against God [as it was for St Paul] but arose from the sensitivity of certain individuals to certain truths of creation suppressed in the wider culture.[5]

The Church should therefore beware of the possibility that in using St Paul and other biblical texts to condemn homosexuality today, it is actually condemning a group of people who embody some profound truths that the Church has lost sight of.

Vasey goes further than this in suggesting that the passionate and often violent clashes between Christians and gay people are so heated precisely because they share so much in common. Both are attempting to resist the idols of contemporary society, both are endeavouring to promote love over hate and violence, both express their deepest feeling and longings in various types of art, both are frequently misunderstood, ridiculed and marginalised. This also explains why so many gay people are drawn to and remain in the Church even though what they find there is a often a 'cruel betrayal' of the gospel to which they so warmly respond. Using St Paul's letters Vasey suggests four possible strategies for the Church. The first is 'missiological pragmatism'. In 1 Corinthians we see St Paul attempting to accommodate the fact that the Roman Empire was not going to go away. He is happy to accept the social ordering of the empire and work with it. The Church could decided that gay people are here to stay and make the sort of accommodation it made to capitalism and its social arrangements. In doing so the Church may find that the presence of gay people within its congregations may ironically help it recognise and resist the idols of modern society. The second is 'the radicalisation of ethnic and social identity'. Taking its cue from Paul's refusal in Galatians to identify Christ with any particular ethnic or gender identity the Church may decide that in the new creation wrought by Christ sexual identity is unimportant. The third possible approach is acceptance without agreement. When Paul addressed disagreements over food laws in Romans he is clear that agreement is not a condition of fellowship, rather it is in a fellowship of mutual acceptance that disagreements must be faced. Finally, in 2 Corinthians where we find Paul trying to restore a broken relationship with the community at Corinth we see him exercising vulnerability before reconciliation. He does not cajole or seek to impose his authority but from a sense of weakness and vulnerability in himself he makes clear that the people at Corinth must come to their own free choice.

Vasey's queer credentials are obvious in his genealogical methodology, his argument is that homosexuality is always a cultural phenomenon and his construction of contemporary western gay culture as in essence a resistance movement, opposing the contemporary construction of masculinity. Along with Foucault Vasey seeks to desexualise homosexuality. It is not chiefly about sex but about modelling a different type of masculinity and a different type of relationship – friendship – which propels gay people into the heart of the Christian tradition. For Vasey, of course, it was not only a valorisation of friendship that gay people share with the ancient Christian tradition, it was also a non-natural, tragic understanding of death and a reconnecting of desire with immortality. Gay people may help the Church recover a vision of heaven for,

> A gay person turning to scripture and the Christian tradition for an image of heaven is in for some pleasant surprises. In heaven there is no marriage (Matthew 22.30; Luke 20.35) ... . The biblical and traditional images of heaven are preoccupied with style and public celebration as to be almost camp. While relentlessly political, they have more in common with a Gay Pride event than with the sobriety of English political life or the leisurewear informality of evangelical Christian life. Again, the vision of heaven is firmly rooted in a present experience of suffering, oppression and exclusion (Revelation 6.9–11; 13.16; 18). The hope of heaven does not rest on fitting in with the way of the world but on the Lion and the Lamb (Revelation 5.5.) – on the beauty of a king who strives for justice and the love of a gentle friend who takes to himself our pain and failure.[6]

In Christ There is No Male or Female

Kathy Rudy, an American theologian, also adopts a genealogical methodology in her theological reflections on gender and homosexuality.[7] She charts the re-ordering of gender that took place in North America during the industrial revolution focussing on the effect it had upon non-working class, white women. Suddenly society was reconstructed and men and women were placed into separate spheres with women relegated to the home, in charge of the cult of domesticity, creating a haven of peace in a competitive world, dependent upon their men for their material needs. The effects upon women were not entirely negative for in their separate spheres where they were encouraged to think of themselves as fundamentally different from men and better at morality and piety, women began to think of themselves as women, organise themselves as women and as fewer children were needed in the towns than in the country they gained greater control over their fertility giving them time and space for political activism. It was many women's involvement in the movement to abolish slavery that led them eventually to become suffragists applying the same principles of equality, justice and liberty to slaves and to themselves. Black women were, of course, still in the work force subjected to exploitation and abuse. Because white women were now identified with piety the Church became their space. As well as baptising the cult of domesticity and making the family a theological rather than economic necessity because everyone needed a mother/wife as the point of contact between themselves and God, the Church also provided a place in which women could exercise authority and leadership particularly in social struggles and reform movements. Industrial capitalism turned women from lustful, weak and sinful creatures, dependent upon their fathers/husbands for their spiritual welfare into the guardians of religion and morality.

Rudy believes that American Christians are still influenced by this construction of gender. Gender still determines what roles may be taken up in churches and the family is still idealised. The Christian Right in particular continues to promote the cult of domesticity. She argues that it is possible to trace the origins of Christian fundamentalism in the States to resistance to the emergence of the New Woman in the early twentieth century who rejected the cult of domesticity. Conservative Christianity preaches now what it preached then, that God is known through gender:

> God remained 'father' in the Cult of Domesticity not because women were inferior or like animals, but rather because women were primarily the people who had relationships with God. Within a system that requires that opposite genders complement each other, if the most spiritual human beings are women, then God, by logic, must be male.[8]

Conservative Christian resistance to inclusive language and gender-neutral imagery for God is based upon awareness that if God is not male then the social construction of gender, the heterosexual family, and gender theology cannot stand.

The Christian Right's campaign for the 'traditional' family includes a fight for sexual 'purity'. In the cult of domesticity women redeemed the lustful nature of sexual desire by enfolding it in romance and making the sexual encounter within marriage a spiritual event. All other forms of sexual activity were regarded as depraved and disordered. Identifying sexual purity and the 'traditional' family with real, original

American culture the Christian Right have since the 1970s fought their campaign in the arena of local, party and national politics. Constructing American culture as one in decline and falling further and further away from its Christian roots, the Christian Right summon America back to purity in order to be ready for the second coming of Christ.

In the 1990s the Christian Right presented gay people as the chief threats to the Christian culture of America. AIDS was constructed as both the inevitable result of and God's punishment on those who because they exist on the margins or outside of the 'traditional' family are immoral and promiscuous. The Christian Right presents gay people as having a disproportionate amount of political power which they are using to undermine the family and American. Gay men and lesbians 'queer' gender and for conservative Christians they thus threaten humanity's ability to have relationship with God because God knows us through gender. Many gay people responded to this discourse by claiming their relationships were marriages and their domestic relationships families and sought legal and ecclesiastical recognition of that fact. Liberal Christian theologians, liberal gay Christian theologians and liberal Christian communities in seeking to resist the violence of the Christian right argued that gay relationships were able to live up to the ideal of heterosexual ones.

Rudy believes that it is unfortunate that gay people have become such good mimics of heterosexual families because other ways and means of organising social relations are never considered. She argues that urban gay male culture often dismissed by straight and gay Christian alike as 'promiscuous' and 'seedy' actually offers an alternative model of social relating in which allegiance to the community, rather than to individuals within it is, is primary. Indeed sex is the means by which men are initiated into the community and the means by which community is built and enforced: 'The church needs the model of gay sexual communities because Christians have forgotten how to think about social and sexual life outside the family'.[9] The result is that the Church has forgotten how to be Church, how to be a community, how to be the Body of Christ and perhaps gay men have the grave task of teaching it how to be a community wider than a family.

Like Vasey Rudy believes it is vital that Christians grasp the cultural construction of same-sex desire and that the concept of a homosexual identity is less than a hundred years old, for the same forces that created separate spheres for men and women also created separate spheres for homosexuals and heterosexuals and drove people into urban centres to earn wages that meant that they could congregate with others of similar desires. Rudy sees an affinity between queer theorists' desire to question and subvert categories of sexual identity and the Christian calling to identify ourselves as the people of God and to reject any other category that divides us:

> Through our baptism we become new people, with a new and radically different ontology; everything that we think and see and do in the world should reflect that we are a part of the Body of Christ. What holds Christians together is not wealth or class status or human-made law or ethnic background or race or nationality, but rather God's self, which is revealed to us through our membership in the Christian Church. Our primary identification is and ought to be Christian; any identification that takes precedence over our baptism is to be avoided.[10]

Christians do not need the categories of gay and straight. Indeed, the current Christian obsession with the 'issue' of homosexuality is distracting the Churches from the more urgent task of thinking about what constitutes moral sex. Furthermore, Rudy suggests Christians do not need the categories of male and female. Christianity does not reproduce itself through biology but through conversion. What matters is not whether two Christians can bear children but whether they can embrace outsiders. Queer theory can help Christians think radically about gender and in return Christianity can challenge queer theory not to jettison God, religion and the spiritual life, things traditionally designated as women's work.

Finally, Rudy attempts to construct a sexual ethic which is communal in nature and queer in its politics. Traditionally Christianity has declared that for sex to be moral it must be unitive – the boundaries between the individuals are blurred and other embraces other. This is because Christians are constantly called to surrender their boundaries in the body of Christ. Sex has therefore to be understood as part of Christian discipleship. Christianity has also traditionally maintained that sex must be open to the conception of new life. In the twentieth century Christian ethicists have resisted the reduction of this to reproduction alone. Reproduction has been replaced by complementarity, the creation of a new social unit of complementary genders, as the other goal of sexual activity. The result has been the loss of a communal dimension to sexual activity and the reinforcement of gender roles and heterosexuality as the ideal form of Christian relationship so that celibacy, singleness and communal life which have been valued for most of Christian history no longer have a place in Christian life.

Rudy is not impressed by the efforts of lesbian feminist theologians to respond to this construction by emphasising the unitive dimension of sexuality alone and identifying it with the mutuality. She takes the Foucauldian view that power never be dissolved, it is everywhere. She also thinks that lesbian feminism has not really appreciated the fact that culture forms our desire and what in one culture might be experienced as violence in other may not. Because of her adoption of queer theory Rudy also has no time for the view that gay people have some epistemological privilege in the discourse on sexuality. The same question faces all Christians: how can sex be used to entrench us in the body of Christ? For Rudy the story of Sodom teaches us that what is ultimately pleasing to God about sexuality is the quality of its hospitality. This is not to say that every stranger must be offered sex but that sex must cultivate an openness and warmth to strangers, it must open our hearts, break down our boundaries, and push us beyond ourselves. Hospitality is procreative, it expands and widens the community. When we open our homes to outsiders, the private space of the home becomes the public space of the Church and so not only is gender collapsed but so is the dualism between private and public. The cult of domesticity is destroyed and replaced by an ethic which subverts worldly concepts of gender and understands sex in the context of building up the body of Christ.

Bodies Before God

Eugene F. Rogers Jr like Rudy is concerned to centre the Body of Christ in a Christian theological discourse on sexuality and like Vasey he refers little to queer theory but finds within traditional Christian theology the tools for a radical critique of modern discourses on sexuality.[11] He wishes to re-orientate the Church debate on 'homosexuality' away from the concepts of heterosexuality and homosexuality towards baptism and marriage. Like Rudy Rogers focuses on the issue of identity and the theological necessity of putting ecclesial identity first. At and through baptism, according to ancient Christian theology, a Christian changes his or her citizenship and in the process the new citizens of the city of God become resident aliens in the world. All other identities are secondary. Reflecting upon the baptismal formula in Galatians 3.28 Rogers asserts, 'The most important thing for Christians to learn from this book is not about sexuality, but about how they should Christianly construe their relationship to God, and the most important lesson to learn there is simply *that they are Gentiles*'.[12] By which he means that all of us who are Christian but not Jewish are dependent upon God's gracious willingness to graft Gentiles onto the vine of Israel. This realisation was as much a shock to Paul as to his opponents in the circumcision debate because for both Gentiles were regarded as morally inferior by nature, as were women and slaves. Galatians 3.28 demands that the burden of proof for exclusion from the ecclesial community and its sacraments must always lie with those who would exclude.

> The Gentile Church … has no God of its own. It worships another God, a God strange to it, the God of Israel, and Gentile Christians are strangers within the their gate. Gentiles, even Gentile Christians, are not God's first love, not those of whom God is jealous, not those to whom God is betrothed, with whom God has made and renewed a covenant. Gentiles are so foreign to the God of Israel that Paul can say that God acts 'contrary to nature', *para phusin*, in grafting them in.[13]

Paul's use of this phrase in Romans 11.14 is shocking considering his previous use of the phrase earlier in this letter to describe, not homosexual people, but Gentiles who characteristically engage in same-sex activity, a characteristic that distinguishes them, not from heterosexuals, but from the Jews. Rogers points out that by Romans 11 Paul is making the outrageous claim that God stands in solidarity with these Gentiles, God like them acts against, or more accurately, in excess of nature, 'Just as God saved flesh by taking it on and defeated death by dying, here God saves those who act in excess of nature by an act in excess of nature'.[14] Without erasing the distinction between gay and straight anymore than that between Jew and Gentile the Church must be open to the possibility that God is pouring his spirit out upon lesbian and gay people. For if he does not then the salvation of all Gentile Christians (i.e. the vast majority of us) may be at stake.

The conferring of a subversive baptismal identity is not the end of the story. Christians must be moulded into the shape of Christ. For Rogers this involves a recovery of marriage and monasticism for all regardless of sexual orientation, as the means by which the ecclesial community, the body of Christ will be built up. Indeed, for Rogers, marriage is properly theologically understood as a form of denial and restraint, an asceticism and therefore

> the trouble with most conservative accounts is not that in denying same-sex couples the rite of marriage they would deny them true-self satisfaction, although they might. The trouble is that in denying same-sex couples the rite of marriage they would deny them true self-denial.[15]

Both marriage and monasticism build up the body of Christ by practising hospitality to the stranger (usually a child in heterosexual marriage) and the married need the monastic to remind them that the purpose of sex is the taking up of the human body into the life of God. Echoing Vasey Rogers argues that the celibate saves Christianity from the grave mistake of believing that sexual love reaches its end, its fulfilment in sexual pleasure or procreation rather than God. Rogers is not persuaded by those gay and lesbian theologians who advocate the model of friendship for lesbian and gay sexual relationships because friendship does not provide the stability necessary for the sanctification process. Monasticism is also a form of marriage. The tradition makes this clear, ascetics are married to God. Both forms of asceticism require time and intensity. Furthermore if, as John Chrysostom claims, in marriage the partners participate in the life of the Trinity because marriage is the form of Christ's relationship to the Father, marriage is part of each Christian's baptismal identity. Incorporating lesbian and gay people into marriage would be to incorporate them into the *kenosis* that Christ demonstrated to the Church and to incorporate them into the practice of Christian hospitality which, though it may not manifest itself in terms of procreation, will still welcome the stranger as the great monastic same-sex communities have always done.

In a typically queer move Rogers then turns to the tradition and to two theologians who have often been dismissed by lesbian and gay people as 'homophobic' – Thomas Aquinas and Karl Barth. In Aquinas Rogers finds a hermeneutical strategy based upon a community formed by a text which requires multiple readings of a text which in turn creates the space for that community to consider 'disputed questions'. This pre-modern approach to the text resonates with the postmodern conviction that texts are unstable. In Barth Rogers finds a doctrine of Israel's election which is intimately related to marriage. Using these two classic theologians Rogers constructs a theology of sexuality. God is like a wedding feast, two being witnessed to, celebrated and supported by a third and therefore God can make a marriage an image of the Trinity as Richard of St Victor argued. Much of the doctrine of the Trinity's power derives from

> the ambiguity – even gender bending – of its symbolics. God as the Trinity without reference to persons can, in traditional Christian exegesis, both require masculine pronouns and 'be our Mother', God is Father but not male; Jesus is Mother but not female; the Spirit is male, female, or neuter depending on language, and also denied to have gender ... . Analogy is more flexible than to require that one occupy a gender to represent it. Unlike, therefore, most uses of divine marriage, the Trinity resists sharp definitions of gender and denies the image of the fertile union of a private two.[16]

The Trinity is an eternal dance, a perichoresis, of grace. The Father eternally sends out the son and receives him back and the Spirit eternally delights and celebrates this movement. Creation, the result of God's good pleasure and eternal nature, generates the very possibility of marriage because it allows for the movement of the dance of grace under the conditions of finitude. There is no procreative principle enshrined in the Trinity, both Augustine and Richard St Victor explicitly reject the idea that the Spirit is the child of the Father and Son. Sex's primary purpose is sanctification, the creation of the children of God. Furthermore, the whole pattern of adoption, ingrafting, and resurrection, which goes to the heart of God's extension of the covenant to the Gentiles, transfigures procreation, insisting that all human beings (that is, Jew and Gentile) find fulfilment in sanctification, that is, in God.[17]

Therefore the 'family resemblance' by which same-sex partnerships may be called marriages is nothing to do with the issue of procreation but their resemblance to the union between Christ and his Church and this, indeed, is the only reason why opposite-sex unions may be justifiably called marriages.

Thus although Rogers tends to assume the existence of a stable homosexual subject as a *theological* rather than social construction because to be a 'person' is important theologically, for personhood invokes an analogy with the personhood of the Trinity, he nevertheless ends up dissolving the difference between gay and straight in that analogy and in the marriage/monasticism in which it is played out.

Beyond Resentment

James Alison, an English Catholic theologian believes that a problem with gay theology is its fragmentary and reactive nature. What gay people have to learn to do, Alison argues, is 'inscribe our lives into the biblical story, inhabit the biblical universe'. This story is not one of reaction, it is a story of 'being called into being and rejoiced in'.[18] Alison finds the discourse of 'coming out' unsatisfactory from a theological standpoint because it is a narrative of conversion which ends rather than begins a story:

> The real drama of the coming-out experience is precisely that it is the beginning of a taking of positions in the midst of something like a lynch mob, and the discovery that by taking position I become not a 'gay man', whatever that might be, but a real participant in the life of the human race, just as I am, warts and all. But it is also a realisation that my previous failure to stand up for the weak was not simply neutral, but left me in collusion with violence.[19]

The theological difference is the same as that between the Reformer's doctrine of justification and that espoused by the Council of Trent. Trent allowed for the possibility of penance. In the Eucharist the Church celebrates the real presence of Christ who gives us the power to become penitent,

> to undo our ways of being bound in by the powerful paternity of the world, and to become able to relate to each other as weak brothers and sisters, ones of no account, who are coming to be held in being by the apparently weak, but ultimately powerful creative love of the Father who is.[20]

For Christians, creation and resurrection are the same doctrine. For the resurrection brings to an end a false paternal understanding of creation and inaugurates an understanding of the fatherhood of God in which we are created as children. When gay people finally accept this, when, in other words, they fully embrace their baptismal identity they will no longer feel resentful towards the Church because they will have let go of their 'indignant and tense identities' and be anxious to reach out towards brothers and sisters who have not yet heard the good news. Alison begins the process of inscribing gay people into God's story through some powerful reflections and retellings of biblical stories. For example, he retells the story of the Gerasene demoniac as a story of the creator 'peacefully calling to life those who have been trapped by the violence of cultural belonging'[21] by collapsing the group through humanising the 'bad' guy. Developing an awareness of being a child and heir of the Father frees people from the rivalry of having to try to belong, of seeking approval, of caring what other people think and thus anger can collapse and bigotry be dispelled. Alison does not reflect upon queer theory nor does he touch upon issues of gay identity in any depth but he does question the formation of a gay identity based upon resentment and anger and suggests, as most queer theologians do, that the baptismal identity at least relativises and at best dissolves modern constructions of sexual identity replacing them with a far more significant identity as a child and heir of the Father.

Radical Orthodoxy

Radical orthodoxy is a loose theological tendency that developed in Britain in the 1990s. Most of its adherents are Roman or Anglo Catholics and it is essentially a Catholic theological response to both the challenges and opportunities posed to theology by postmodernism. Its radical nature lies in both its return to patristic and medieval tradition and a determination to engage with contemporary issues. It is orthodox in its commitment to creedal Christianity and patristic theology. It is a movement of theological mediation rejecting both the neoorthodox distrust of human reason in the theological enterprise and Roman Catholic doctrinalism. Radical orthodoxy has as its heart the Augustinian belief that all knowledge is divine illumination and the Platonic notion of participation which denies the existence of any realm beyond God and therefore beyond the interest or concern of theology. Theology must be concerned with the body and sexuality and engage with contemporary critical theory because whilst the tradition must not be rejected, it does need rethinking. However, these discourses are always suspended by transcendence which interrupts them, exposing their weaknesses and nudging them towards a greater truth. Radical orthodoxy takes advantage of the break down of the metanarratives of modernism to claim a voice and a space for Christian epistemology and for the re-enchantment of the world.[22]

One of the most prominent British theologians in this school is Graham Ward, Professor of Contextual Theology and Ethics at the University of Manchester. His essay on the displaced body of Jesus Christ will suffice as an example of radical orthodoxy's embrace and use of queer theory.[23] Ward sets out to reflect upon the gendered body of Jesus as scripture presents it and as the Church has reflected upon it from the perspective of the ascension with the intention of arguing that

> Since none of us has access to bodies as such, only to bodies that are mediated through the giving and receiving of signs, the series of displacements or assumptions of Jesus' body continually refigures a masculine symbolics until the particularities of one sex give way to the particularities of bodies which are made and female.[24]

Ward is interested in the performance of Jesus 'the gendered Jew' and the way that the performance has been scripted and re-performed by the Church.

The body of Jesus is from the moment of its incarnation present, in the sense that it is gendered and performs its gender within the social context of its time and place. It is also backward looking to a pre-fallen corporeality and eschatological in that it looks forward to the resurrection. Jesus is born male but from purely female matter, he emerges from the womb in a complex web of symbolic relationships with his virgin mother.

> The baby boy is husband and bridegroom, spouse and prefigured lover of the mother who gives him birth, whose own body swells to contain the future Church. The bridal chamber is the womb which the bridegroom will impregnate with his seed while also being the womb from which he emerges. The material orders are inseparable from the solid and transcendent orders, the orders of mystery. The material orders are caught up and become significant only within the analogical orders. And so here Jesus' body is brought within a complex network of sexualised symbolic relations that confound incest and the sacred.[25]

The body of the baby Jesus is stretched, pre-figuring the crucifixion (at his circumcision), resurrection and the creation of the ecclesial body. The instability of the body is further played out in the displacements of the transfiguration, the Eucharist, the resurrection and finally the ascension. In the transfiguration, the body of Christ becomes transparent to divinity – our attraction to this figure is taken through the male gendered Jew through to the second Adam which he is revealed to be, towards God in whom desire is finally satisfied. In the Eucharist, Jesus' body is transposed, extended into the gender neutral form of bread and, as Ward notes, bodies are revealed as things not only transfigurable but also transposable and 'in being transposable, while always being singular and specific, the body of Christ can cross boundaries, gender boundaries for example. Jesus' body as bread is no longer Christ as simply and biologically male'.[26] In the crucifixion and death, Jesus' body becomes liminal and soaked in iconicity, it becomes a floating signifier which the medieval Church could represent as a maternal body, the side wound representing a womb from which the Church springs.

The resurrection recapitulates and plays out all previous displacements, revealing the body as essentially mysterious and beyond grasp because the body is finally transposed into the Church at the ascension. Jesus becomes the multi-gendered body of the Church. As the revealer of true humanity, Jesus reveals this because all bodies are situated within and given significance within his body. They too are 'permeable, transcorporeal and transpositional'.[27] Christian living then becomes a participation in this 'permeable, transcorporeal and transpositional' body in an individual and corporate arena. Feminist theologians who have been vexed by the issue of whether a man can save a woman and gay theologians who have speculated on the sexuality of Jesus have, according to Ward, simply failed to understand the nature of the body of Christ.

Although Ward makes only one explicit reference to Butler in this essay, the queerness of his analysis is obvious. Ward's point is that the pre-modern Christian tradition was itself queer and this is played out in its constructions of the body of Jesus. Materiality, gender and sexual identity are drawn attention to and then dissolved in the body of Jesus and as members of the body of Christ, Christians participate in that process themselves.

Trans-Gendered

Virginia Ramey Mollenkott has recently be prompted to reconsider the nature of gender by reading Leslie Feinberg's novel *Stone Butch Blues* which deals with working class American lesbians in the early days of gay liberation.[28] For Mollenkott, who identifies herself in this book as 'somewhat transgendered', the ultimate reason for queerness does not lie in social theory but in God who chooses to incarnate him/ herself in diverse ways which explode the gender binary divide. Transgendered people (by which Mollenkott means a whole collection of sexual outlaws including intersexed people, transsexual people, cross-dressers, androgynes, drag artists and gay and lesbian and bisexual people) in their own persons expose the social construction of gender. Like most other queer theologians Mollenkott believes the Christian tradition to be essentially queer in its attitude to identity. Genesis 2.21–24 suggests that the original human creature was non-gendered, the Virgin Birth of Christ recalls that original creature, the Church as the body of Christ is omnigendered, boundaries between all social groups subverted and blurred. The Church has canonised many saints among them Saints Pelagia, Marina, Eugenia, Anastasia and, of course, Joan of Arc who have defied gender roles and in some cases crossed them, growing beards and other 'male' accessories. John Milton envisaged a queer heaven with angels shifting genders and engaging in 'immortal nuptial's and 'joyous revels'. Like the radical orthodoxy school Mollenkott understands the project of returning to this queer tradition to be about the enchanting of the world by crossing boundaries and in the process erasing them. This is the stuff of magic.

Positively Indecent

Marcella Althaus-Reid is an Argentinian theologian who lectures in Christian Ethics and Practical Theology at the University of Edinburgh. In her work queer theory meets liberation theology, postcolonialist and post-Marxist theory in order to produce what Althaus-Reid calls an indecent theology.[29] An indecent theology is a theology that draws attention to and subverts sexual and gender codes something that liberation theology has signally failed to do. Althaus-Reid's genealogical critique is largely focussed on theology and the mechanisms of exclusion that have been operative in Latin American liberation theology. When the poor process with a statue of Mary through the *fabelas* demanding jobs then liberation theologians recognise this as a part of the manifestation of God's option for the poor but when from the same *fabela* a festival procession includes a transvestite Christ and a drag queen Mary Magdalene liberation theologians do not even see them. It has done nothing to challenge the Latin American system of decency which regulates gender behaviour. This is because liberation theology, for all its radicalness, has still been under the control the of North American and European production line of theology. Feminist liberation theology has been done through the eyes of women but not through their sex. Althaus-Reid is suspicious of the use of the Virgin Mary in feminist liberation theology which does not deal with the inscription of gender and sexuality that this theological symbol produces and reinforces upon women's bodies. The result is what she calls 'vanilla theology', theology which does not question the dominant scripts of womanhood and sexuality or the use of the Marian symbol by dictatorial regimes. If God, Mary and Jesus cannot be queered/made indecent, if we cannot talk about Mary Queer of Heaven or God/Jesus the faggot then there is little point in doing theology because God, Jesus and Mary would only have meaning within a heterosexual economic system. Among the urban poor of Latin America Santa Librada is a popular figure of devotion – she is a cross between Jesus and Mary, a saint of ambiguous gender, bearing a resemblance to Mary but crucified like Christ, she is the patron of those on the run from the police. She represents for Althaus-Reid a transvestite epistemology which is common among the urban poor in Latin American but never reflected in liberation theology.

For Althaus-Reid theology must become obscene is it is to be a theology of grace, for it must dis-cover and expose flesh and materiality. The black Christ is obscene because he exposed racism. The Christa which represents Christ as female on the cross is obscene because she uncovers sexism and heterosexism. Like Goss, Althaus-Reid constructs a 'systematically deviant Jesus', an obstinate friend of sinners and of prostitutes.[30] Like Vasey she foregrounds a Christ outside the gates who is eternally the Bi/Christ who always gives us something to think about, disrupting our discourses. Christ's resurrection is a resurrection of lust, the passion and vivacity of one who knew love refused to die. He was a Messiah who constantly exceeded the space of the Messiah.

Althaus-Reid's theology is a theology which 'outs' the heterosexuality of the dominant discourses of liberation theology. She demonstrates that not all queer theology leads its exponents back to traditional doctrine, she shares the lesbian feminists distrust of traditional doctrine and though she cites the theo-practices of the urban poor in their devotion to 'queer' saints and queering of Mary and Jesus her work is largely deconstructive rather than constructive.

Queering Theology

Queer theology though still young and sparse has developed a number of distinctive characteristics. First it rejects a metaphysics of substance: gender and sexual identities are deconstructed and they are deconstructed through baptismal incorporation to the body of Christ. For, second, queer theologians tend to argue that Christian theology was queer two thousand years before queer theory was invented and this is particularly evident in the constructions of the body of Jesus and the Trinity. Third, most of the queer theology produced so far takes advantage of the break down of the metanarratives to attempt to re-enchant the world. If sexuality is unstable so is all 'reality' and doctrines and stories which liberal theology might reject as irrational suddenly become believable again. It is a shame that queer theology came too late in the AIDS crisis to be motivated to respond to the articulation of life after death among those dying. For queer theology with its relentless, obstinate deconstruction of all binary divides would surely have no problem destabilising the boundaries between life and death. Queer theology though it usually begins with issues of sexuality is not really 'about' sexuality in the way that gay and lesbian theology is about sexuality. Queer theology is actually about theology. In gay and lesbian theology sexuality interrogated theology, in queer theology, theology interrogates sexuality but from a different place than modern theology has traditionally done, the place of tradition. Queer theology denies the 'truth' of sexuality and hence declares that it is not stable enough to build a theology upon. Althaus-Reid's approach is the exception here and she tends to utilise queer theory in much the same way that early liberation theologians utilised Marxist theory, as a tool to analyse experience. In her work experience still seems to be primary and therefore it would be better to characterise her work as liberation theology informed by queer theology than as queer theology as such.

Queer theory we must remember is not without its critics. It has been accused of patriarchal terrorism boring its way into gender politics and erasing the hard fought identities of women and gay men in the name of liberation. It has also tended towards nihilism, the only hope it can hold out is the hope of an unending subversive performance of identity, an endless drag show. And, perhaps most importantly, for many who are sympathetic to its aims as a project it seems hopelessly idealistic. It is fine as a theory but where are the spaces and incentives in most of our lives to perform gender subversively? Queer theology has to address these concerns.

Notes

1   Mark Vernon, '"I am not what I am" – Foucault, Christian Asceticism and a "Way Out" of Sexuality', in Jeremy R. Jeremy Carrette (ed.), *Religion and Culture by Michel Foucault* (Manchester: Manchester University Press, 1999), p. 208.
2   Vasey, *Strangers and Friends*, p. 95.
3   Vasey, *Strangers and Friends*, p. 176.
4   Vasey, *Strangers and Friends*, p. 177.
5   Vasey, *Strangers and Friends*, p. 140.
6   Vasey, *Strangers and Friends*, p. 248.
7   Kathy Rudy, *Sex and the Church: Gender, Homosexuality and the Transformation of Christian Ethics* (Boston: Beacon Press, 1997).
8   Rudy, *Sex and the Church*, p. 38.
9   Rudy, *Sex and the Church*, p. 78.
10 Rudy, *Sex and the Church*, p. 97.
11 Eugene F. Rogers Jr, *Sexuality and the Christian Body: Their Way into the Triune God* (Oxford and Malden, 1999).
12 Rogers, *Sexuality and the Christian Body*, p. 50.
13 Rogers, *Sexuality and the Christian Body*, p. 64.
14 Rogers, *Sexuality and the Christian Body*, p. 65.
15 Rogers, *Sexuality and the Christian Body*, p. 70.
16 Rogers, *Sexuality and the Christian Body*, p. 197.
17 Rogers, *Sexuality and the Christian Body*, p. 208.
18 James Alison, *Faith Beyond Resentment: Fragments Catholic and Gay* (London: Darton Longman and Todd, 2001), pp. 196–7.
19 Alison, *Faith Beyond Resentment*, p. 201.
20 Alison, *Faith Beyond Resentment*, p. 204.
21 Alison, *Faith Beyond Resentment*, p. 130.
22 See John Milbank, Catherine Pickstock and Graham Ward (eds), *Radical Orthodoxy: A New Theology* (London and New York: Routledge, 1999), pp. 1–21 and John Milbank, 'The Programme of Radical Orthodoxy', in Laurence Paul Hemming (ed.), *Radical Orthodoxy? A Catholic Enquiry* (Aldershot: Ashgate, 2000), pp. 33–45.
23 Graham Ward, 'Bodies: The Displaced Body of Jesus Christ', in Milbank, Pickstock and Ward (eds), *Radical Orthodoxy*, pp. 163–81.

24 Ward, 'Bodies', p. 163.
25 Ward, 'Bodies', pp. 164–5.
26 Ward, 'Bodies', p. 168.
27 Ward, 'Bodies', p. 176.
28 Virginia Ramey Mollenkott, *Omnigender: A Trans-Religious Approach* (Cleveland: The Pilgrim Press, 2001).
29 Marcella Althaus-Reid, *Indecent Theology: Theological Perversions in Sex, Gender and Politics* (London and New York: Routledge, 2001).
30 Althaus-Reid, *Indecent Theology*, pp. 112–13.

Chapter 8

Christianity is a Queer Thing

Theological Exhaustion

Imagine a wrestling match where the last person standing wins the prize. At first the competitors are keen, fierce and committed to the fight, they do not give each other an inch. Then as time rolls on they start to get tired and their energy lags, but when one competitor makes a clever move, the other is fired up by indignation and retaliates and so the fight goes on. But eventually paralysing weariness overcomes both wrestlers and they slump down before one another. Neither is prepared to admit defeat, too much is at stake, so they continue to maintain a token grasp upon one another. Unable to let go and unable to resolve the situation, they are trapped by the rules of the game. This situation is a bit like the state of the current debate on homosexuality in western Christianity. The debate has rumbled on for the best part of 30 years, sometimes fiercely, and now is in a stalemate born of the plain exhaustion of going around and around in circles, repeating the same old arguments. This stalemate is testimony to the theological inadequacy of the arguments of all sides in the debate. We have reached a state of theological breakdown. It was Vasey's genius to realise that the inadequacy of the theology stemmed from an embrace by all involved of modern notions of sexual identity. For gay and lesbian people their sexual identity tells the truth about who they are and so to exclude them from the Church or from any of its offices or functions on the grounds of sexual orientation is to deny their full personhood and is therefore a theological offence. Their opponents identify Christian discipleship with heterosexuality in various ways (in some Churches a person's stance on homosexuality has become a test of orthodoxy) but mostly in the very modern (and Protestant) identification of Christian discipleship with heterosexual marriage and bourgeois family life. In each case the concepts of gender and sexual identity remain unchallenged and simply assumed. Even those who may go so far as to question the existence of homosexuality except as a pathological deviation from heterosexuality, as some Evangelicals do, seldom question the 'reality' of heterosexuality or gender. Gay and lesbian theology made the mistake of putting its ultimate trust in the traditions of modernity rather than the traditions of Christianity with the result that it has sometimes ceased to be recognisable as theology at all, and forfeited its place in contemporary Christian dialogue because it no longer speaks the same language nor does it follow the same 'grammatical' rules as its opponents. It has been unable to cope with the questioning of some of the central concepts of modernity in the postmodern age.

A Queer Church

Queer theory as a form of divine illumination came along just at the right time to offer some sort of solution to the impasse of the wrestling saints by pulling the rug out from under both of them. It subverted the rules of the game by questioning the notion of gender and sexual identity. But queer theory itself needs disruption from the transcendent to save it from hopeless idealism and nihilism. For there is only one community charged with being queer and that is the Church and it is so charged for a purpose, the preparation of the kingdom of heaven. Only Christianity can make queer theory a viable strategy for only Christians are called to imitate their God in acting *para phusin*, in excess of nature.

Rudy noted that it is by baptism and not biology that one enters the Church. Rowan Williams points out that baptism constitutes a ritual change of identity, a setting aside of all other ordinary identities in favour of an identity as a member of the body of Christ.[1] A queer theorist, like Alison Webster, might want to respond by arguing that surely Christian identity is as unstable or slippery as a sexual identity, a mere matter of performance as well?[2] But Williams argues that it is not. What we receive in baptism is not an identity negotiated in conversation with our communities or culture such as our sexual and gender identities are; it is an identity over which we have no control whatsoever. It is sheer gift. In the sixteenth century Lancelot Andrews pointed out that the presence of the Trinity at baptism reminds us of creation which was a purely gratuitous gift, and baptism constitutes a new creation equally gratuitous.[3] It is God's great 'yes' to us based not upon our own merits but upon divine love revealed in Christ. The nature of elements of our Christian identity may be obscure to us and how we best act out our identity in our various contexts might be a legitimate subject of dispute but the identity itself is not negotiated, it is given.

Baptism, according to Williams, exposes the place outside of it as a place of loss and need.[4] In particular the 1662 Book of Common Prayer baptismal rite (which is the basis of Williams' reflections) understands baptism as a movement from enslavement to desires which will destroy us because they drive us to, 'objects that fill gaps in our self-construction, so that what we desire is repletion, which is immobilisation, a kind of death' to a realisation that all desire has its proper end in the divine, 'we must receive the grace to want the endlessness of God'.[5] In other words baptism reveals the inadequacy of all other forms of identity and the desire caught up in them and therefore, 'the rite requires us *not* to belong to the categories we thought we belonged in, so that a distinctive kind of new belonging can be realised'.[6] This new belonging is based upon a solidarity that we have not chosen and is grounded in a radical equality that comes from all being there through grace alone, a grace which, Rogers reminds us, comes in the form of an unnatural act on the part of God, an unnatural act that deconstructs the whole notion of the 'natural' for evermore.

Baptist theologian Timothy Bradshaw reflecting on the use of baptism in some recent radical theology has pointed out the fact that baptism does involve a death – a death to self, sin and to the ultimacy of certain types of identity.[7] Bradshaw believes that baptism arguments are dangerous ones for 'radicals' precisely because the New Testament emphasises the discontinuity of baptism, 'participation in this new life is transformed and challenging, life in the tension of the already but not yet'.[8] Gay and lesbian theology when it has drawn upon the theology of baptism usually fails to appreciate this discontinuity. So Marilyn Bennett Alexander and James Preston in their book, *We Were Baptised Too*[9] argue that the Churches, by marginalising lesbian and gay people and depriving them of certain sacraments such as ordination, have reneged on the promise made to them at their baptism to support their lives in Christ. It is a clever argument but one that does not appreciate the really radical nature of the Christian understanding of baptism. For the Church has always taught that baptism changes a person in the depths of their very being, which it is why that change is described as a new creation brought about through a death to sin and also, in the Catholic tradition, described as the bestowal of a character which configures the baptised to Christ so that their very selves are united to Christ through the Church. What Alexander and Preston have not grappled with is that at baptism the ontology of the baptised is radically changed, they become what might be called ecclesial persons. This personhood is characterised by a new subjectivity which is communal and corporate, for it both shares in and constitutes the body of Christ, the new human. The Church, though in a constant struggle against the power of sin, nevertheless testifies to and anticipates a new humanity in which human beings 'coalesce indissolubly into a single existence' with Christ.[10] This is why the Council of Trent could state,

> For, in those who are born again, there is nothing that God hates; because, there is no condemnation to those who are truly buried together with Christ by baptism into death; who walk not according to the flesh, but, putting off the old man, and putting on the new who is created according to God, are made innocent, immaculate, pure, harmless, and beloved of God, heirs indeed of God, but joint heirs with Christ; so that there is nothing whatever to retard their entrance into heaven. But this holy synod confesses and is sensible, that in the baptized there remains concupiscence, or an incentive (to sin); which, whereas it is left for our exercise, cannot injure those who consent not, but resist manfully by the grace of Jesus Christ; yea, he who shall have striven lawfully shall be crowned. This concupiscence, which the apostle sometimes calls sin, the holy Synod declares that the Catholic Church has never understood it to be called sin, as being truly and properly sin in those born again, but because it is of sin, and inclines to sin.[11]

The baptised manifest a new type of creaturehood/humanity, one in which sin has no ultimate hold. It is still perfectly possible to act sinfully but sin no longer has the power to alienate humanity from God. The baptised belong to another world. To be baptised is to be caught up in a kingdom that does not yet fully exist, that is in the process of becoming, it is to be caught up in the redemption of this world.

It is not that the baptised are called to live beyond culture, which is impossible and undesirable because the Spirit is active in human culture, but that they are called to transform it by living in it in such a way as to testify to the other world being born within it. All our cultural identities are placed under eschatological erasure. Heterosexuality and homosexuality and maleness and femaleness are not of ultimate importance, they are not determinative in God's eyes and in so far as any of us have behaved as if they are we are guilty of the grave sin of idolatry and if we have further behaved as if they are grounds upon which to exclude people from the glorious liberty of the children of God we are guilty of profanity and a fundamental denial of our own baptismal identity which rests in being bound together with others not of our choosing by an act of sheer grace.

Culture is humanity's contribution to creation, the means by which we strive to perfect nature. But sin distorts our vision, there is many a slip between the cities we build and the city of God and yet the spirit is active within our creations, prompting and subverting. Sexual and gender identities have to be subverted because they are constructed in the context of power and are part of a matrix of dominance and exclusion. They grate against the sign of baptism. This is not to say that on a non-ultimate level these identities may not have some use and been mediations of God grace, for indeed they have. We have already seen how categories of sexuality identity have been used by lesbian and gay people to subvert the very assumptions that led to their creation in the first place. In giving some people a new and strong sense of self they enabled men and women within the context of philosophical and theological liberalism and liberation to expose and challenge assumptions about same-sex desire. Feminism similarly took the category of woman, exposed its patriarchal construction and then reinvested it with meaning. These were all movements of grace but in themselves they are not complete and by their inadequacy we are led back to the theology of baptism which demands something even more radical from Christian theologians, a questioning of the very categories of identity themselves.

Christians are then called to live out their culturally negotiated identities in such a way as to expose their non-ultimacy, to take them up into the processes of redemption. They do this by parodying them. Parody is not a simple sending up. Linda Hutcheon defines parody as 'an extended repetition with critical difference' which has 'a hermeneutical function with both cultural and even ideological implications'.[12] Parody has long been the habitual Christian modus operandi. I am writing this chapter on a Sunday. A few hours ago I celebrated the Eucharist which is itself an extended repetition with critical difference of the Last Supper, the critical difference being that in the Eucharist the meal element is caught up in a new reality, the reality of the heavenly liturgy opened up to us through by the cross and resurrection. The Last Supper itself was probably an extended repetition with critical difference of the Seder meal, the critical difference being the inauguration of a new covenant and the creation of a new community called to live out the outrageous hospitality of God. As David Ford has noted, improvising on a theme, non-identical repetition, is intrinsic to the Christian faith which 'is true to itself only by becoming freshly embodied in different contexts .... Theologically understood, they [such repetitions] are testimony to God's creativity and abundance ... . They show the particularising activity of the Holy Spirit – a flourishing of distinctive and different realisations of the eventfulness of God'.[13] Modernity's quest for identical repetitions evident in the banality of mass-produced goods or in the dangerous quest of fundamentalism to endlessly reproduce the 'original' text or meaning in every age and context demonstrates a lack of faith in and understanding of the Spirit. Parody is then the Christian way of operating, of taking what is given to us and playing it out in such a way as to expose the other world breaking through it.

Earlier generations of Christians were much better at parodying gender than us. The prominence given to the religious life in a Catholic context right up until the mid twentieth century was crucial to the parodic performance of maleness and femaleness. The vowed celibate testified to two ultimate truths. The first is that heterosexuality, marriage and family life are not identical with Christian discipleship. How could they be when Augustine constructed heterosexual relations as inessential but the consequence of the fall. The second is that all desire is ultimately orientated towards God. Our desire for the other is ultimately desire for the Other and will not be satisfied until it reaches its *telos*, its end in God. The decline of and increasing invisibility of the religious life in western Christianity constitutes a huge crisis for the Church in general and for its discourse on sexuality in particular. It is both a product of and has contributed towards the collapse of Christian discipleship into heterosexual marriage. In public discourse on sexuality the western Churches currently give every impression of wanting to produce heterosexual desire rather than desire for God and contemporary society does not need yet another agency producing such desire. The immensely popular 'Seeing Salvation' millennium exhibition at the National Gallery in London contained a number of pictures of Christ exposing his wounds to Thomas or to other disciples. The imagery was most certainly erotic but the erotic gaze was diverted from the genitals, imparting the message that ultimately human desire could only be fulfilled through the wounds of Christ, through God's sheer gift of himself. The vowed celibate in their own person testifies to the *telos* of desire. They further testify to the end of history inaugurated by the birth of the Christ child – the perfect human being – and by his death and resurrection which together dissolve the need for human beings to reproduce because the perfect child has been born and in the resurrection which he inaugurated all will be re-membered and remembered and so the need for heirs is cancelled. The celibate also parodies singleness living without a partner but with a critical difference, the critical difference being that in the Church no one is actually single, no one is alone, all are bonded together in the body of Christ. One of the reasons for the crises we have witnessed among religious and the celibate priesthood in recent years is that the Church as a body has left them alone, has forgotten how to nurture and love them, has failed to take responsibility for them. And one of the reasons for this forgetting is the Church's idealisation of marriage and family life.

The religious life has also traditionally been a place in which cultural constructions of maleness and femaleness have been parodied, at least in part. Celibates became 'mothers' and 'fathers' in their communities presiding over groups in which a new type of kinship, no longer based upon blood relationships, united people as 'brothers' and 'sisters'. In my youth it was common for religious women to be known by men's names. The queering was not perfect because it did not usually work the other way round (although there is a tradition in some male religious communities of referring to the male superior as 'mother') but nevertheless it was a queering nonetheless. Growing up surrounded by men wearing clothes society labelled feminine whom I had to relate to as 'father', taught by women who were my 'sisters' or 'mothers' with names such as Augustine and Bernard Joseph taught me that societal categories were not fixed, that they could be played around with and that the Church was a space in which gender shifted.

Thomas Laqueur has demonstrated that until the Enlightenment western culture constructed female bodies as imperfect inversions of male bodies. There may have been different genders but there was one sex. This allowed for the possibility of flux and change, a possibility which was closed off in the Enlightenment period when male and female bodies were sharply differentiated as a reaction to the earliest forms of feminism.[14] Mollenkott has drawn attention to the rich tradition of gender bending in Christian hagiography. This tradition was, of course, constructed in the context of patriarchy so the transitions tend to be female to male. Maleness was identified in much early Christian discourse with perfect humanity and femaleness with fallen humanity. Some early Church fathers taught that women could become 'manly' by exercising virtue and actually become models of manliness for men.[15] Even though manifesting many patriarchal assumptions these traditions nevertheless undermine one of the central props of patriarchy by constructing gender as fluid and therefore as lacking in ultimacy.

In the writings of the early Church father and ascetic, Gregory of Nyssa, a number of theologians have identified a queer theologian who predates Butler by hundreds of years. Gregory in his reflections on the resurrection constructs a body which is fluid. Unlike some early theologians Gregory does not associate change with decay but with movement towards the next life. Reading Genesis 1.27 with Galatians 3.28 Gregory argued that the original human creature was not sexed and it was to this angelic pre-lapsarian state that human beings would return in the resurrection. This state can to some extent be anticipated in the ascetic life and indeed was in the body of Gregory's sister Macrina who is portrayed as performing both male and female roles. Gregory describes her as going 'beyond' the nature of a woman which, for Gregory, does not mean that she had reached manly perfection but rather that she was anticipating in her own body redeemed and restored humanity. For Gregory as the soul ascends to God it moves from an active courting of Christ as 'Sophia' (therefore taking a 'male' role) to a passivity in which it is the bride embraced by Christ the bridegroom.[16] It became common in the Christian tradition and in Christian art to represent the soul as female to represent the ultimate nuptial relationship between the soul and God. Gregory then looks to a life beyond gender which can be anticipated in this life.

Lost Horizons

Sarah Coakley sees in Butler's programme of gender trouble and in the whole queer project an unconscious 'gesturing to an eschatological horizon which will give mortal flesh final significance, a horizon in which the restless, fluid post-modern "body" can find some sense of completion without losing its mystery, without succumbing again to "appropriate" or restrictive gender roles'.[17] Foucault perceived a common cause between queer theologians and ancient ascetics and it is becoming increasingly obvious that in the marginalisation of the monastic tradition within contemporary Christianity the Church has cut itself off from a radical sexual discourse, an ancient form of queer theory which often needs to be read through the lens of feminism to counter its patriarchal assumptions but which nevertheless anticipates queer theory and provides an answer to its pessimistic nihilism.

In chapter 3 I noted that the Church, even whilst it has condemned same-sex relationships, has nevertheless manufactured same-sex desire through its liturgy and devotional system. This desire has been focussed on Christ (represented as both male and female) but also produced in the context of the idealisation of same-sex (specifically male) friendship which was sometimes given liturgical expression in the form of sworn brotherhood.[18] In this tradition there is something eschatological about same-sex friendship, it anticipates the kingdom of heaven in a manner marriage cannot because marriage ends at death. Bray notes that in memorials to sworn brothers it is common for the friends to be depicted under canopies like saints, suggesting the continuation of their brotherhood in the resurrection.[19] The late Cardinal Basil Hume in a note on homosexual people in the Catholic Church also drew attention to the eschatological dimension of all friendship:

> When two persons love, they experience in a limited manner in this world what will be their unending delight when one with God in the next. To love one another is in fact to reach out to God who shares his loveableness with the one we love. To be loved is to receive a sign, or a share, of God's unconditional love.[20]

The production of same-sex desire whether between the worshipper and Christ or two between friends was part of the Church's production of desire for God. In a hetero-patriarchal context in which relations between men and women are tightly structured and the difference between the sexes emphasised, same-sex friendship was often understood to anticipate a reality beyond the present in which relationships are denaturalised, disordered and refocused.

From the author of Ephesians 5 who constructs the male Christ with a female body – the Church- so that men who belong to the body of Christ are part of a female body and yet the Church as a whole is called to be Christ to the world, therefore requiring women to be part of a male persona, again and again in Christian writings gender is played out and broken open in order to better reveal the nature of the redeemed, ecclesial person. What is remarkable is how little this tradition has impacted upon contemporary discussions on sexuality within western Christianity. In chapter five we noted that gay and lesbian theology failed to deal with the theological issues thrown up by AIDS and this could be attributed at least it part to its indebtedness to liberal and liberationist forms of theology which have usually ignored or demythologised eschatology. The loss of an eschatological imagination, not just in gay and lesbian theology, but across much of western Christian theology has impoverished Christian discourse on sexuality and has allowed the collapse of desire into heterosexuality and discipleship into marriage and modern constructions of the family. The Church has lost sight of its ultimate horizon when discussing sexuality and gender.

In a book she wrote several years after *Gender Trouble* Judith Butler suggested that in modernity 'I' is predicated on the foreclosure of certain forms of desire with the result that the subject is grounded in melancholia and shrouded in an unacknowledged and irresolvable grief for impossible love, for to acknowledge it would mean the destruction of the self. Both heterosexuality and homosexuality are dependent upon each other for their existence but that dependence is based upon repudiation of the desire each identity rests upon. Gender and sexual identity are then a kind of melancholy.[21] This melancholia expresses itself in a number of ways including the association of non-heterosexuals with death. David Sollis' interviews with those living with HIV/AIDS and with those who had seen thousands of men to their graves revealed that for many of these men their funerals were consciously constructed as a performance of their identity as gay men. For some their funeral provided the only opportunity they would have to celebrate their sexuality in a public and liturgical rite. Most of them were adamant that they wanted their funerals to be light-hearted affairs at which people laughed rather than cried. These funerals were also often planned to be occasions of camp excess. The nature of camp is disputed within gay and lesbian and queer studies but some of the basic characteristics of camp include a desire to trivialise that which society deems serious, as a way of acknowledging and deconstructing its seriousness, a strong sense and celebration of artifice, and an excess, an extravagance of performance.[22] Philip Core defined camp as 'the lie that tells the truth',[23] because a surplus of meaning is produced in a camp performance that reveals the instability and artificiality of that which is being performed. In the funeral services of many men with AIDS a spectacle is created which draws attention to the deceased's sexual identity but at the same time is often so 'over the top', so exaggerated that the sexual identity is exposed as an artifice and the humour that defies the grief and melancholia also ironically serves to draw attention to that which is defied and anticipates a place beyond the melancholia of gender. In these funeral services we encounter a push not only beyond death but also a place beyond gender and sexual identity. What AIDS appears to have done (unnoticed by most gay and lesbian theologians) is to lead not just to a reconnection between desire and immortality (as Vasey anticipated) but to a reconnection between immortality and the dissolving of gender and sexual identity.

From the Christian tradition we learn that Butler's diagnosis of melancholia can only be dealt with in two ways: through the eschatological deconstruction of gender (which can be anticipated now) and in the perfection and fulfilment of desire in God. It is in the Eucharist that the baptised learn about and anticipate the eschatological life. It is, as Cardinal Joseph Ratzinger has noted, a rehearsal of the life to come, a form of play in which we learn about and prepare for a life 'which St Augustine describes, by contrast with life in this world, as a fabric woven, no longer of exigency and needed, but of the freedom of generosity and gift'.[24] In the Eucharist Christians gather and face eastwards towards the rising sun, towards the risen and returning Christ. They also face the cosmos, for the Eucharist is a Eucharist of the Church living and departed. In the Eucharist the Church stands on the edge of heaven and standing on the edge of heaven gender differences dissolve. All face the same way. In the pre-Vatican II Catholic rite the priest too faced east. One of the unfortunate results of the introduction of the Eucharist *versus populum* is that it draws attention to the gender of the priest in a manner that the old rite did not. Nevertheless the confining of the priesthood or any other liturgical ministry to one gender grates again the sign of baptism and the eschatological dimension of the Eucharist. Confining any order, ministry or role to one gender or sexual orientation (or to one race or class) solidifies rather than dissolves non-eschatological reality. It signifies a lack of an eschatological horizon. At the consecration of the elements the Church learns again and again of the instability, fluidity and transposable nature of the body. In the Eucharist the Church reconstitutes itself as the bride of Christ and the body of Christ. Desire is refocused on the divine. The intercourse is between Christ and humanity. Feminism made the abolition of exclusive language – whether used of God or of the Church – one is its primary aims and rightly so because the use of one set of gender language further solidifies gender and helps to create and reinforce structures of exclusion. However, the use of gender specific language can in fact help the process of queering. Culturally constructed forms of identity cannot hold much power over those women who are used to being addressed as 'brothers' or men who are forced to understand themselves as the brides of Christ.

One, Holy, Catholic and Apostolic

It is in the Eucharist too that the Church learns what it is called to be and it is in this context that theological reflection on sexual morality must be done, because for the baptised their personhood primarily is an ecclesial one. The Church is called first to be one. As Rudy noted the Church has a long tradition of affirming that sexual relationships must be unitive which is to say that they break the boundaries of the self and propel people out of individualism into *koinonia*. While any sexual encounter can temporarily break the boundaries of the self, the Christian aim is to achieve a permanent porousness which can only be achieved with considerable practice – lifelong practice in fact – and therefore requires stability and a presumption of permanence on behalf of the couple and the community around them. In his film *The Opposite of Sex* (1998) Don Roos poses the question 'what if sex is not about reproduction or recreation but concentration?' St Augustine had a strong awareness of the inability of the human will to stay focused; it was too easily distracted and dissipated. Marriage should school the will and desire to concentrate and focus as part of the preparation for the eternal concentration on God. But this should not distract us from the fact that Christians are not called into a sexual community but an ecclesial one. We are not called primarily into coupledom but into the body of Christ. Sexual relationships must themselves be permeable to the Church and spill over into the Church. Only if our relationships build up the body of Christ by proclaiming the gospel and challenging the Church to be faithful to that gospel can they be deemed to be truly unitive.

The Church is called to be holy. We say that something is holy when we recognise what John Milbank has called the 'heavy pressure of the divine on finite reality'.[25] And divine reality is sheer grace, an excessive giving that creates the possibility of reciprocity and mutuality not mere exchange. Grace is returned to God by being passed on, by sustaining the momentum of God's giving and the Church is both constituted by the gift and caught up in the divine act/being of giving.[26] Within the Christian tradition marriage and monasticism have been presented as two paths to holiness. Rogers noted that both monasticism and marriage are ascetic practices in which human love is taken up into the divine and through which we participate in the excess of God's giving by learning to love and through offering hospitality to strangers. Indeed Rodney Clapp has argued that Christians have only have children so 'we can become the kind of people who welcome strangers'.[27] Since gender and sexual identification have no ultimate significance in Christian theology, marriage cannot be understood as a heterosexual institution any more than monasticism can because heterosexuality does not 'really' (i.e. eschatologically) exist. Those who, in the cultural constructions of our day are labelled lesbian and gay are entitled to the same paths of holiness as everyone else and all are entitled to have the path of monasticism recommended to them with as much warmth and effort as the Church currently encourages marriage. Indeed, both monasticism and same-sex marriages are necessary for the holiness of the Church, to remind it that gender is not of ultimate concern and that desire has an end beyond human relationships. The Church also needs to recover its long tradition of valorisation of friendship along side monasticism and marriage. The formation of friendships is part of the larger project of learning to embrace the stranger but friendship also serves to break the bonds of culturally constructed kinship and the captivity of passion within sexual relationships. Friendship keeps the eschatological dream alive by breaking love out of coupledom, by breaking love out of the confines of sexual orientation, and sometimes by outlasting other forms of love.

The Church is called to be Catholic. Avery Dulles in his study of the catholicity of the Church draws attention to the textured meaning of the term 'catholic'. It suggests organic unity: firmly centred but nevertheless dynamic and spilling out in difference. Catholicity is manifest primarily in the Godhead itself and both the universe and the Church derive their catholicity from God.[28] Sexual relationships must be conducted not in the context of the modern liberal discourse on sexuality or in the bourgeois family but in a broader catholic context of the internal relations of the Godhead which spills out into community of the Church and returns to itself.

Finally, the Church is called to be an apostolic institution, that is an institution that stands in a dynamic tradition and in a communion of saints. It is also an institution that understands itself as a community under authority. Christian sexual relations are never private affairs in the Church. They take place within a context of a living tradition and have to be understood and worked out within the context of that tradition. At the moment the Church needs to recover its queer tradition in order to resolve the crisis it is in over homosexuality and because it needs to recover an eschatological vision. But we are always at risk of betraying the story. As Michael Jinkins has noted, the same word *paradidomi* is used in the New Testament to refer to the handing on of tradition and the handing over of Jesus in an act of betrayal.[29] The Word in becoming flesh, in becoming an open sign, makes itself vulnerable to betrayal. This is why the Church has every right to question the way we conduct our lives, why we as Church keep ourselves in relationship with our foreparents in faith, allowing them to continue to challenge and cajole us and why we often need the intervention of the divine from outside the immediate Christian context through other forms of knowledge to return us to a more faithful interpretation of tradition. An awareness of an apostolic identity should encourage a positive and deep engagement with the Christian tradition on the one hand and an appropriate humility in all of us, which should manifest in a willingness to consider the possibility that we might be wrong. Dante's vision of purgatory should serve as a reminder that all human desire is disordered by sin, which was St Augustine's great realisation, and though it propels us towards the love that moves the sun and the stars it can only take us to the edge of heaven. In the end we are all in the same boat. In the end we may all be wrong about issues of sexuality.

In the End

In the end gay is not good, straight is not good, no one is good but God alone and redemption does not come through gender or sexuality rather these are taken up into the process of redemption. The Church as the community of the redeemed must play out gender and sexuality in such a way as to reveal their lack of eschatological significance. In the end as my body lies in its casket before the altar my hope will lie not in my sexual orientation, or my gender but my baptism and my family and friends rightly absorbed into the wider ecclesial community at that moment will be reminded that this is their only hope as well. The Church could learn a lot from its funeral services. If I am very lucky I may already be on the seventh cornice of purgatory, for the first time ever enjoying a run, purging my desire so that it becomes properly focused but grateful that it has brought me thus far, to the very edge of bliss.

My hope is that the kiss of peace which Dante's souls exchanged in passing might yet be anticipated in this life and queer theology might have the necessary theological integrity, being grounded as it is in Christian tradition, to create an atmosphere in which Christians who have been so bitterly divided by issues of sexuality might be propelled into an embrace that comes from a realisation that we have all put our faith in the wrong thing, in sexuality rather than God.

Notes

1 Rowan Williams, *On Christian Theology* (Oxford and Malden: Blackwell, 2000), p. 189.
2 Alison Webster, 'Queer to be Religious: Lesbian Adventures Beyond the Christian/Post-Christian Dichotomy', *Theology and Sexuality* 8 (March 1998), pp. 27–39.
3 Kenneth Stevenson, *The Mystery of Baptism in the Anglican Tradition* (Norwich: Canterbury Press, 1998), pp. 56–61.
4 Williams, *On Christian Theology*, p. 209.
5 Williams, *On Christian Theology*, p. 211.
6 Williams, *On Christian Theology*, p. 209.
7 Timothy Bradshaw, 'Baptism and Inclusivity in the Church', in Stanley E. Porter and Anthony R. Cross (eds), *Baptism, the New Testament and the Church: Historical and Contemporary Studies in Honour of R.E.O. White* (Sheffield: Sheffield Academic Press, 1999), pp. 458–9.
8 Bradshaw, 'Baptism and Inclusivity in the Church', p. 461.
9 Marilyn Bennett Alexander and James Preston, *We Were Baptised Too: Claiming God's Grace for Lesbians and Gays* (Louisville: Westminster John Knox Press, 1996).
10 Joseph Ratzinger, *Die sakramentale Begründung christlicher Existenz* (Feising: Kyrios, 1973).
11 *The Canons and Decrees of the Sacred and Oecumenical Council of Trent*, ed. and trans. J. Waterworth, (London: Dolman, 1848), pp. 23–4.
12 Linda Hutcheon, *A Theory of Parody: The Teaching of Twentieth-Century Art Forms* (New York: Methuen, 1985), pp. 2–7.
13 David Ford, *Self and Salvation: Being Transformed* (Cambridge: Cambridge University Press, 1999), p. 144.
14 Thomas Laqueur, *Making Sex: Body and Gender from the Greeks to Freud* (Cambridge: Harvard University Press, 1990).
15 Gillian Cloke, *This Female Man of God: Women and Spiritual Power in the Patristic Age, AD 350–450* (London and New York: Routledge, 1995).
16 See, for example, Sarah Coakley, 'The Eschatological Body: Gender, Transformation, and God', *Modern Theology* 16.1 (January 2000), pp. 61–73 and Verna Harrison, 'Male and Female in Cappadocian Theology', *Journal of Theological Studies* 41 (1990), pp. 441–71.
17 Coakley, 'The Eschatological Body: Gender, Transformation, and God', p. 70.
18 Boswell, *The Marriage of Likeness* and Alan Bray, 'Friendship, the Family and Liturgy: A Rite for Blessing Friendship in Traditional Christianity', *Theology and Sexuality* 13 (September 2000), pp. 15–33.
19 Interview with David Sollis in Sollis, *Queering Death*, pp. 166–7, 173.
20 Cardinal Basil Hume, 'A Note on the Teaching of the Catholic Church Concerning Homosexual People', 6 March 1995.
21 Judith Butler, *The Psychic Life of Power* (Stanford: Stanford University Press, 1997), pp. 132–50.

22 Susan Sontag, 'Notes on "Camp"', in Fabio Cleto (ed.), *Camp: Queer Aesthetics and the Performing Subject: A Reader* (Edinburgh: Edinburgh University Press, 1999), pp. 53–65.
23 Philip Core, *Camp: The Lie that Tells the Truth* (London: Plexus, 1984).
24 Joseph Cardinal Ratzinger, *The Spirit of the Liturgy* (San Francisco: Ignatius Press, 2000), p. 14.
25 John Milbank, *The Word Made Strange: Theology, Language Culture* (Oxford: Basil Blackwell, 1997), p. 131.
26 Stephen H. Webb, *The Gifting God: A Trinitarian Ethics of Excess* (Oxford and New York: Oxford University Press, 1996).
27 Rodney Clapp, *Families at the Crossroads: Beyond Traditional and Modern Options* (Downers Grove: InterVarsity Press, 1993), p. 138.
28 Avery Dulles, *The Catholicity of the Church* (Oxford: Clarendon Press, 1985).
29 Michael Jinkins, 'De-Scribing Church: Ecclesiology in Semiotic Dialogue', *Scottish Journal of Theology* 51 no 2. (1998), pp. 188–213.

Bibliography

Abelove, H., Barale, M.A. and Halperin, D.M. (eds), *The Lesbian and Gay Studies Reader* (New York: Routledge, 1993).

Alexander, M. Bennett and Preston, J., *We Were Baptised Too: Claiming God's Grace for Lesbians and Gays* (Louisville: Westminster John Knox Press, 1996).

Alison, J., *Faith Beyond Resentment: Fragments Catholic and Gay* (London: Darton, Longman and Todd, 2001).

Althaus-Reid, M., *Indecent Theology: Theological Perversions in Sex, Gender and Politics* (London and New York: Routledge, 2001).

Barth, K., *Church Dogmatics*, III.4 (Edinburgh: T and T Clark, 1960).

Boswell, J., *Christianity, Social Tolerance and Homosexuality: Gay People in Western Europe from the Beginning of the Christian Era to the Fourteenth Century* (Chicago: University of Chicago Press, 1980).

———, *The Marriage of Likeness: Same-Sex Unions in Pre-Modern Europe* (London: HarperCollins, 1994).

Bradshaw, T., 'Baptism and Inclusivity in the Church', in Porter, S.E. and Cross, A.R. (eds), *Baptism, the New Testament and the Church: Historical and Contemporary Studies in Honour of R.E.O. White* (Sheffield: Sheffield Academic Press, 1999), pp. 447–66.

Bray, A., *Homosexuality in Renaissance England* (London: Gay Men's Press, 1982).

———, 'Friendship, the Family and Liturgy: A Rite for Blessing Friendship in Traditional Christianity', *Theology and Sexuality*, 13 (September 2000), pp. 15–33.

Bristow, J., *Sexuality* (London and New York: Routledge, 1997).

Brooten, B.J., *Love Between Women: Early Christian Responses to Female Homoeroticism* (Chicago and London: University of Chicago Press, 1996).

Butler, J., *Gender Trouble: Feminism and the Subversion of Identity* (London and New York: Routledge, 1990).

———, *The Psychic Life of Power* (Stanford: Stanford University Press, 1997).

The Canons and Decrees of the Sacred and Oecumenical Council of Trent, ed. and trans. Waterworth, J. (London: Dolman, 1848).

Clapp, R., *Families at the Crossroads: Beyond Traditional and Modern Options* (Downers Grove: InterVarsity Press, 1993).

Clark, J.M., *A Place to Start: Toward an Unapologetic Gay Liberation Theology* (Dallas: Monument Press, 1989).

———, *A Defiant Celebration: Theological Ethics and Gay Sexuality* (Garland: Tangelwüld Press, 1990).

———, *Beyond Our Ghettos: Gay Theology in Ecological Perspective* (Cleveland: The Pilgrim Press, 1993).

———, *Defying the Darkness: Gay Theology in the Shadows* (Cleveland: The Pilgrim Press, 1997).

Cleaver, R., *Know My Name: A Gay Liberation Theology* (Louisville: Westminster John Knox Press, 1995).

Cloke, G., *This Female Man of God: Women and Spiritual Power in the Patristic Age, AD 350–450* (London and New York: Routledge, 1995).

Coakley, S., 'The Eschatological Body: Gender, Transformation, and God', *Modern Theology*, 16.1 (January 2000), pp. 61–73.

Comstock, G.D., *Gay Theology Without Apology* (Cleveland: The Pilgrim Press, 1993).

———— and Henking, S. (eds), *Que(e)rying Religion: A Critical Anthology* (New York: Continuum, 1999).

Congregation for the Doctrine of the Faith, *Letter to the Bishops of the Catholic Church on the Pastoral Care of Homosexual Persons* (London: Catholic Truth Society, 1986).

Core, P., *Camp: The Lie that Tells the Truth* (London: Plexus, 1984).

Dante, *The Divine Comedy 2: Purgatory*, Canto XXVI (Harmondsworth: Penguin Books, 1955).

D'Emilio, J., *Making Trouble: Essays on Gay History, Politics and the University* (New York: Routledge, 1992).

Dulles, A.,*The Catholicity of the Church* (Oxford: Clarendon Press, 1985).

Edwards, T., 'The AIDS Dialectics: Awareness, Identity, Death, and Sexual Politics', in Plummer, K. (ed.), *Modern Homosexualities: Fragments of Lesbian and Gay Experience* (London and New York: Routledge, 1992), pp. 151–9.

Ford, D., *Self and Salvation: Being Transformed* (Cambridge: Cambridge University Press, 1999).

Fortunato, J.E., *Embracing the Exile: Healing Journeys for Gay Christians* (San Francisco: Harper and Row, 1982).

————, *AIDS: The Spiritual Dilemma* (San Francisco: Harper and Row, 1987).

Foucault, M., *The History of Sexuality, Volume 1: An Introduction* (New York: Random House, 1978).

Fulkerson, M. McClintock, *Changing the Subject: Women's Discourses and Feminist Theology* (Minneapolis: Fortress Press, 1994).

————, 'Gender – Being it or Doing It? The Church, Homosexuality, and the Politics of Identity', in Comstock, G.D. and Henking, S.E. (eds), *Que(e)rying Religion: A Critical Anthology* (New York: Continuum, 1999), pp. 188–201.

Gearhart, G. and Johnson, W.R. (eds), *Loving Women/Loving Men: Gay Liberation and the Church* (San Francisco: Glide Publications, 1974).

Gilson, A. Bathurst, *Eros Breaking Free: Interpreting Sexual Theo-Ethics* (Cleveland: The Pilgrim Press, 1995).

Glaser, C., *Come Home! Reclaiming Spirituality and Community as Gay Men and Lesbians* (San Francisco: Harper and Row, 1990).

————, *Coming Out as Sacrament* (Louisville: Westminster/John Knox Press, 1998).

Goss, R., *Jesus Acted Up: A Gay and Lesbian Manifesto* (San Francisco: HarperSanFrancisco, 1993).

————, 'The Beloved Disciple: A Queer Bereavement Narrative in a Time of AIDS', in Goss, R.E. and West, M. (eds), *Take Back the Word: A Queer Reading of the Bible* (Cleveland: The Pilgrim Press, 2000), pp. 206–18.

Harrison, V., 'Male and Female in Cappadocian Theology', *Journal of Theological Studies*, 41 (1990), pp. 441–71.

Heyward, C., *Speaking of Christ: A Lesbian Feminist Voice* (New York: The Pilgrim Press, 1984).

————, *Touching Our Strength: The Erotic as Power and the Love of God* (San Francisco: Harper and Row, 1989).

————, *When Boundaries Betray Us: Beyond Illusions of What is Ethical in Therapy and Life* (San Francisco: HarperSanFrancisco, 1993).

————, *Saving Jesus From Those Who Are Right: Rethinking What it Means to be a* Christian (Minneapolis: Fortress Press, 1999).

Hume, B., 'A Note on the Teaching of the Catholic Church Concerning Homosexual People', 6 March 1995.

Hunt, M.E., *Fierce Tenderness: A Feminist Theology of Friendship* (New York: Crossroad, 1991).

Hutcheon, L., *A Theory of Parody: The Teaching of Twentieth-Century Art Forms* (New York: Methuen, 1985).

Jagose, A., *Queer Theory: An Introduction* (New York: New York University Press, 1996).

Jinkins, M., 'De-Scribing Church: Ecclesiology in Semiotic Dialogue', *Scottish Journal of Theology*, 51 no 2. (1998), pp. 188–213.

Jones, C., *Stitching a Revolution: The Making of an Activist* (San Francisco: HarperSanFrancisco, 2000).

Jordan, M., *The Silence of Sodom: Homosexuality in Modern Catholicism* (Chicago and London: University of Chicago Press, 2000).

Kwok, Pui-Lan, 'The Future of Feminist Theology: An Asian Perspective', *The Auburn News* (Fall, 1992), n.p.

Lacan, J., *Speech and Language in Psychosis* (Baltimore: Johns Hopkins University Press, 1981).

Laqueur, T., *Making Sex: Body and Gender from the Greeks to Freud* (Cambridge: Harvard University Press, 1990)

Lathrop, G., '"O Taste and See": The Geography of Liturgical Ethics', in Anderson, B.E. and Morrill, B.T. (eds), *Liturgy and the Moral Self: Humanity at Full Stretch Before God* (Collegeville: Minnesota, 1998), pp. 41–54.

Libânio, J.B., 'Hope, Utopia, Resurrection', in Sobrino, J. and Ellacuría, I. (eds), *Systematic Theology: Perspectives from Liberation Theology* (London: SCM, 1996), pp. 279–90.

Lindbeck, G., *The Nature of Doctrine, Religion and Theology in a Postliberal Age* (Philadelphia: Westminster Press, 1984).

Long, R.E., 'God Through Gay Men's Eyes: Gay Theology in the Age of AIDS', in Long R.E. and Clark, J.M., (eds), *AIDS, God and Faith: Continuing the Dialogue* (Dallas: Monument Press, 1992), pp. 1–22 and 27–36.

Lorde, A., 'Uses of the Erotic: The Erotic as Power', in Nelson, J.B. and Longfellow, S.P. (eds), *Sexuality and the Sacred: Sources for Theological Reflection* (London: Mowbray, 1994), pp. 75–9.

Macourt, M. (ed.), *Towards a Theology of Gay Liberation* (London: SCM Press, 1977).

May, M., *A Body Knows: A Theopoetics of Death and Resurrection* (New York: Continuum, 1995).

McFague, S., *Models of God: Theology for an Ecological, Nuclear Age* (Philadelphia: Fortress Press, 1987).

———, *The Body of God: An Ecological Theology* (London: SCM, 1993).

McNeill, J.J., *The Church and the Homosexual* (Kansas City: Sheed, Andrews and McMeel, 1976).

———, *Taking a Chance on God: Liberating Theology for Gays, Lesbians, and their Lovers, Families and Friends* (Boston: Beacon Press, 1988).

———, 'The Gay Response to AIDS: Becoming a Resurrection People', *The Way*, 28.4 (October 1988), pp. 330–38.

———, *Freedom, Glorious Freedom; The Spiritual Journey to the Fullness of Life for Gays, Lesbians and Everybody Else* (Boston: Beacon Press, 1995).

Milbank, J., *The Word Made Strange: Theology, Language Culture* (Oxford: Basil Blackwell, 1997).

———, 'The Programme of Radical Orthodoxy', in Hemming, Laurence Paul (ed.), *Radical Orthodoxy? A Catholic Enquiry* (Aldershot: Ashgate, 2000), pp. 33–45.

———, Pickstock, C. and Ward, G. (eds), *Radical Orthodoxy: A New Theology* (London and New York: Routledge, 1999).

Mitulski, J., 'Ezekiel Understands AIDS: AIDS understands Ezekiel or Reading the Bible with HIV', in Goss, R.E. and West, M. (eds), *Take Back the Word: A Queer Reading of the Bible* (Cleveland: The Pilgrim Press), pp. 153–60.

Mollenkott, V. Ramey, *Sensuous Spirituality: Out from Fundamentalism* (New York: Crossroad, 1993).

————, *Omnigender: A Trans-Religious Approach* (Cleveland: The Pilgrim Press, 2001).

Morrison, T., 'Bodies, Sex, Wholeness and Death', in Stuart, E. et al., *Religion is a Queer Thing: A Guide to the Christian Faith for Lesbian, Gay, Bisexual and Transgendered People* (London and Herndon, Va.: Cassells, 1997), pp. 122–3.

Murphy, T. and Poirier, S. (eds), *Writing AIDS: Gay Literature, Language and Analysis* (New York: Columbia University Press, 1997).

Namaste, K., '"Tragic Misreadings": Queer Theory's Erasure of Transgender Subjectivity', in Beemyn, B., and Eliason, M. (eds), *Queer Studies: A Lesbian, Gay, Bisexual and Transgender Anthology* (New York and London: New York University Press, 1996), pp. 183–203.

O'Neill, C and Ritter, K., *Coming Our Within: Stages of Spiritual Awakening for Lesbians and Gay Men* (San Francisco: HarperSanFrancisco, 1992).

Order of Christian Funerals (London: Geoffrey Chapman, 1990).

Pinsent, P., '"My Joy, My Love, My Heart": Sexuality and the Poems of George Herbert', in Hayes, M.A., Porter, W., and Tombs, D. (eds), *Religion and Sexuality* (Sheffield: Sheffield Academic Press, 1998), pp. 135–44.

Rambuss, R., *Closet Devotions* (Durham and London: Duke University Press, 1998).

Ratzinger, J., *Die sackramentale Begründung christlicher Existenz* (Feising: Kyrios, 1973).

————, *The Spirit of the Liturgy* (San Francisco: Ignatius Press, 2000).

Richards, T.A. and Folkman, S., 'Spiritual Aspects of Loss at the Time of a Partner's Death from AIDS', *Death Studies*, 21 (February 1997), pp. 527–52.

Rieger, J.,*God and the Excluded: Visions and Blindspots in Contemporary Theology* (Minneapolis: Fortress Press, 2001).

Rogers, E.F., *Sexuality and the Christian Body: The Way into the Triune God* (Oxford and Malden: Blackwell, 1999).

Rudy, K., *Sex and the Church: Gender, Homosexuality and the Transformation of Christian Ethics* (Boston: Beacon Press, 1997).

Ruether, R. Radford, *Gaia and God: An Ecofeminist Theology of Earth Healing* (New York: Harper Collins, 1992).

————, 'Ecofeminism and Healing Ourselves, Healing the Earth', *Feminist Theology*, 9 (May 1995), pp. 61–2.

Sandfort, T., Schuyf, J., Duyvendak, J.W. and Weeks, J. (eds), *Lesbian and Gay Studies: An Introductory, Interdisciplinary Approach* (London: Sage Publications, 2000).

Sands, K.M., *Escape from Paradise: Evil and Tragedy in Feminist Theology* (Minneapolis: Augsburg Fortress Press, 1994).

Schneider, B. and Stoller, N., *Women Resisting AIDS* (Philadelphia: Temple University Press, 1995).

Sedgwick, E. Kosofsky, *Epistemology of the Closet* (Berkeley: University of California Press, 1990).

Sontag, S., 'Notes on "Camp"', in Cleto, F. (ed.), *Camp: Queer Aesthetics and the Performing Subject: A Reader* (Edinburgh: Edinburgh University Press, 1999), pp. 53–65.

Spencer, D.T., *Gay and Gaia: Ethics, Ecology, and the Erotic* (Cleveland: The Pilgrim Press, 1996).

Steinberg, L., *The Sexuality of Christ in Renaissance Art and in Modern Oblivion* (New York: Pantheon, 1983).

Stevenson, K., *The Mystery of Baptism in the Anglican Tradition* (Norwich: Canterbury Press, 1998).

Stuart, E., *Just Good Friends: Towards a Theology of Lesbian and Gay Relationships* (London: Mowbray, 1995).

———, *Spitting at Dragons: Towards a Feminist Theology of Sainthood* (London: Mowbray, 1996).

———, 'Sex in Heaven: The Queering of Theological Discourse on Sexuality', in Davies, J. and Loughlin, G. (eds), *Sex These Days: Essays on Theology, Sexuality and Society* (Sheffield: Sheffield Academic Press, 1997), pp. 184–204.

——— with Braunston, A., Edwards, M., McMahon, J. and Morrison, T., *Religion is a Queer Thing: A Guide to the Christian Faith for Lesbian, Gay, Bisexual and Transgendered People* (London and Herndon, Va.: Cassell, 1997).

Taylor, M.C., *Altarity* (Chicago: University of Chicago Press, 1987).

Thistlethwaite, S. Brooks, *Sex, Race and God* (London: Geoffrey Chapman, 1990).

Vasey, M., *Strangers and Friends: A New Exploration of Homosexuality and the Bible* (London: Hodder and Stoughton, 1995).

Vernon, M., '"I am not what I am" – Foucault, Christian Asceticism and a "Way Out" of Sexuality', in Carrette, Jeremy R. (ed.), *Religion and Culture by Michel Foucault* (Manchester: Manchester University Press, 1999), pp. 199–210.

Webb, S., *The Gifting God: A Trinitarian Ethics of Excess* (New York and Oxford: Oxford University Press, 1986).

Webster, A., 'Queer to be Religious: Lesbian Adventures Beyond the Christian/Post-Christian Dichotomy', *Theology and Sexuality*, 8 (March 1988), pp. 27–39.

Weeks, J., *Coming Out: Homosexual Politics in Britain from the Nineteenth Century to the Present* (London: Quartet Books, 1977).

Williams, R., *On Christian Theology* (Oxford and Malden: Blackwell, 2000).

Wilson, N., *Our Tribe: Queer Folks, God, Jesus and the Bible* (San Francisco: HarperSanFrancisco, 1995).

Winquist, C.E., *Desiring Theology* (Chicago and London: University of Chicago Press, 1995).

Wolfe, S.J., and Penelope, J. (eds), *Sexual Practice, Textual Theory: Lesbian Cultural Criticism* (Cambridge: Blackwell, 1993).

Woodhead, L., 'Sex in a Wider Context', in Davies, J and Loughlin, G. (eds), *Sex These Days: Essays on Theology, Sexuality and Society* (Sheffield: Sheffield Academic Press, 1997), pp. 98–120.

Yingling, T., 'AIDS in America: Postmodern Governance, Identity, and Experience' in Fuss, D. (ed.), *Inside/Out: Lesbian Theories, Gay Theories* (New York and London: Routledge, 1991), pp. 291–310.

Theses

Malcolm Stuart Edwards, 'Christianity and the Subversion of Identity: Theology, Ethics and Gay Liberation', PhD Thesis, Cambridge University, 1998.

David Sollis, 'Queering Death: A Theological Analysis of the Reconnection of Desire and Immortality in the Shadow of AIDS', PhD Thesis, King Alfred's College, Winchester, 2002.

Websites

http:www.avert.org
http:www.Phls.co.uk
http://www.queertheory.com
http://www.theory.org.uk

Index